AVID

READER

PRESS

Dedicated

THE CASE FOR
COMMITMENT IN AN AGE
OF INFINITE BROWSING

Pete Davis

Avid Reader Press

NEW YORK   LONDON   TORONTO   SYDNEY   NEW DELHI

AVID READER PRESS
An Imprint of Simon & Schuster, Inc.
1230 Avenue of the Americas
New York, NY 10020

First Avid Reader Press hardcover edition May 2021

AVID READER PRESS and colophon are trademarks of Simon & Schuster, Inc.

For information about special discounts for bulk purchases,
please contact Simon & Schuster Special Sales
at 1-866-506-1949 or business@simonandschuster.com.

The Simon & Schuster Speakers Bureau can bring authors to your live event.
For more information or to book an event, contact the
Simon & Schuster Speakers Bureau at 1-866-248-3049 or
visit our website at www.simonspeakers.com.

Interior design by Ruth Lee-Mui

Manufactured in the United States of America

1   3   5   7   9   10   8   6   4   2

Library of Congress Cataloging-in-Publication Data has been applied for.

ISBN 978-1-9821-4090-8
ISBN 978-1-9821-4092-2 (ebook)

To the first two long-haul heroes I met,
Mary Clare Gubbins and Shelton Davis

Not the marvelous act, but the evident conclusion of being.
Not strangeness, but a leap forward of the same quality.
Accomplishment. The even loyalty. But fresh.
Not the Prodigal Son, nor Faustus. But Penelope.
The thing steady and clear. Then the crescendo.
The real form. The culmination. And the exceeding.
Not the surprise. The amazed understanding. The marriage,
Not the month's rapture. Not the exception. The beauty
That is of many days. Steady and clear.
It is the normal excellence, of long accomplishment.

Jack Gilbert, from
"The Abnormal Is Not Courage"

CONTENTS

Contents

Contents

I.

INFINITE BROWSING MODE

1

Two Cultures

Infinite Browsing Mode

You've probably had this experience: It's late at night and you start browsing Netflix, looking for something to watch. You scroll through different titles, you watch a couple of trailers, you even read a few reviews—but you just can't commit to watching any given movie. Suddenly it's been thirty minutes and you're still stuck in Infinite Browsing Mode, so you just give up. You're too tired to watch anything now, so you cut your losses and fall asleep.

I've come to believe that this is the defining characteristic of my generation: *keeping our options open.*

The Polish philosopher Zygmunt Bauman has a great phrase for what I'm talking about: *liquid modernity.* We never want to commit to any one identity or place or community, Bauman explains, so we remain like liquid, in a state that can adapt to fit any future shape.

And it's not just us—the world around us remains like liquid, too. We can't rely on any job or role, idea or cause, group or institution to stick around in the same form for long—and they can't rely on us to do so, either. That's liquid modernity: It's Infinite Browsing Mode, but for everything in our lives.

For many people I know, leaving home and heading out into the world was a lot like entering a long hallway. We walked out of the room in which we grew up and into this world with hundreds of different doors to infinitely browse. And I've seen all the good that can come from having so many new options. I've seen the joy a person feels when they find a "room" more fitting for their authentic self. I've seen big decisions become less painful, because you can always quit, you can always move, you can always break up, and the hallway will always be there. And mostly I've seen the fun my friends have had browsing all the different rooms, experiencing more novelty than any generation in history has ever experienced.

But over time, I started seeing the downsides of having so many open doors. Nobody wants to be stuck behind a locked door—but nobody wants to live in a hallway, either. It's great to have options when you lose interest in something, but I've learned that the more times I jump from option to option, the less satisfied I am with any given option. And lately, the experiences I crave are less the rushes of novelty and more those perfect Tuesday nights when you eat dinner with the friends who you have known for a long time—the friends you have made a commitment to, the friends who will not quit you because they found someone better.

The Counterculture of Commitment

As I have grown older, I have become more and more inspired by the people who have clicked out of Infinite Browsing Mode—the people who've chosen a new room, left the hallway, shut the door behind them, and settled in.

It's the television pioneer Fred Rogers recording 895 episodes of *Mister Rogers' Neighborhood* because he was dedicated to advancing a more humane model of children's television. It's the Catholic Worker founder Dorothy Day sitting with the same outcast folks night after night because it was important that someone was committed to them. It's Martin Luther King Jr.—and not just the Martin Luther King Jr. who confronted the fire hoses in 1963 but also the Martin Luther King Jr. who hosted his thousandth tedious planning meeting in 1967.

As this new type of hero captured my admiration, I started appreciating a different constellation of figures from my childhood than I did at the end of my teenage years. The "cool teachers" faded in my memory—I can't even remember some of their names—but the slow-and-steady ones have lingered.

There was the intimidating stage crew and robotics director from my high school, Mr. Ballou, who built up a student cult of misfit tinkerers and future engineers. He seemed to have a whole wing of the school to himself filled with half-built projects, technology from various decades, and devoted student acolytes clad in matching black T-shirts. Most of the school, myself included, were a bit afraid of him—scared we would get in his way, or worse, break something. But that was the key to his method. If you were willing to face your fears and engage with him, he would train you in any one of the dozens of craft skills he knew.

One time, I made a funny video with my friends for a school variety show. He saw it and told me that I had "absolutely no sense of framing"—and that the video wasn't good enough yet to show to a crowd. My other teachers, just delighted that a student was making something, had always heaped praise on my teenage filmmaking. Mr. Ballou was different. He insisted that if you were going to get into a craft, you should hone it. I remember complaining that he was being a little hard on me.

But the Ballou method cut both ways. Another time, I had the idea of building a concert venue inside the school's junior courtyard. Every teacher thought the idea was ridiculous—*What the heck are you even talking about?* But when I told Mr. Ballou, he wasn't taken aback at all. If I learned the engineering software AutoCAD and designed a blueprint, he told me, he would help me advocate for building it. That's a real teacher—demanding more of you but committing to you if you commit to learning.

I took piano lessons from Mrs. Gatley, who clocked four decades in the same chair next to the same grand piano in her living room on Oak Street. While my other friends got to bop in and out of lessons, one or two years at a time, and learn whichever songs they wanted (Vanessa Carlton's "A Thousand Miles" and Coldplay's "Clocks" were my era's songs), Mrs. Gatley was old school. It wasn't just that her students had to learn their scales and play classical music. By taking lessons with Mrs. Gatley, you were signing up to join an entire immersive experience that was bigger than piano—and bigger than you.

Just taking weekly lessons wasn't allowed—you had to follow the full Gatley calendar with all her other students. There was the fall recital and the Christmas concert, the sonatina festival and the June recital—and each of these events had a corresponding gathering preceding them where every student would prepare together. You had to learn the history of the pianoforte, the difference between the Baroque and the Romantic periods, and the proper way to bow after finishing playing.

You also couldn't really quit. Once, in middle school, I asked Mrs. Gatley if I could take a year off.

"You can, I guess," she responded, "but we don't really take a year off here."

I ended up spending twelve years in the Gatleyverse. As a result, I learned about a lot more than just piano in Mrs. Gatley's living room. I saw what it was like to watch older students play some impossible song—and eventually learn to play it myself. Because Mrs. Gatley knew me for so long, she had the insight and authority to give deeper advice than other teachers, like when she told me: "You move a little fast in life; you might feel better if you slowed down." And when my dad died, it meant something that Mrs. Gatley—who knew him from all the concerts over the years—came to the funeral. You couldn't get that from some one-off teacher who let you play "A Thousand Miles" during the first lesson and quit the first time you got bored.

Folks such as Mrs. Gatley and Mr. Ballou—and icons like Dorothy Day, Fred Rogers, and Martin Luther King Jr.—aren't just a random assortment of people. I've come to think about them as part of a shared counterculture—a Counterculture of Commitment. All of them took the same radical act of making commitments to particular things—to particular places and communities, to particular causes and crafts, and to particular institutions and people.

I say "counterculture" because this is not what today's dominant culture pushes us to do. The dominant culture pushes us to build our résumés and not get tied down to a place. It pushes us to value abstract skills that can be applied anywhere, rather than craft skills that might help us do only one thing well. It tells us to not get too sentimental about anything. It's better, this culture tells us, to stay distant—just in case that thing is sold off or bought out, downsized, or made "more efficient." It tells us to not hold true to anything too seriously—and to not be surprised when others don't, either. Above all, it tells us to keep our options open.

The kinds of people I'm talking about here are rebels. They live their lives in defiance of this dominant culture.

They're *citizens*—they feel responsible for what happens to society.

They're *patriots*—they love the places where they live and the neighbors who populate those places.

They're *builders*—they turn ideas into reality over the long haul.

They're *stewards*—they keep watch over institutions and communities.

They're *artisans*—they take pride in their craft.

And they're *companions*—they give time to people.

They build relationships with particular things. And they show their love for those relationships by working at them for a long time—by closing doors and forgoing options for their sake.

When Hollywood tells tales of courage, they usually take the form of "slaying the dragon"—there's a bad guy and a big moment where a brave knight makes a definitive decision to risk everything to win some victory for the people. It's the man standing in front of the tank, or the troops storming up the hill, or the candidate giving the perfect speech at the perfect time.

But what I've learned from these long-haul heroes is that this isn't the only valor around. It's not even the most important type of heroism for us to model, because most of us don't have to face many dramatic, decisive moments in our lives—at least not ones that spring up out of nowhere. Most of us just confront daily life: normal morning after normal morning, where we can decide to start working on something or keep working at something—or not. That's what life tends to give us: not big, brave moments, but a stream of little, ordinary ones out of which we must make our own meaning.

The heroes of the Counterculture of Commitment—through day-in, day-out, year-in, year-out work—become the dramatic events themselves. The dragons that stand in their way are the everyday boredom and distraction and uncertainty that threaten sustained commitment. And their big moments look a lot less like sword-waving and a lot more like gardening.

The tension

This book is about the tension between these two cultures: the Culture of Open Options and the Counterculture of Commitment. This tension—between browsing the hallway and settling into a room, between keeping our options open and becoming long-haul heroes—exists both inside ourselves as individuals and in society as a whole.

You can find examples of young people acting like browsers all around us. We have trouble committing to relationships, endlessly swiping through potential partners. We uproot ourselves often, jumping from place to place searching for the next best thing. Some of us don't commit to a career path because we're worried that we will be stuck doing something that doesn't quite fit our true self.

Others of us are forced from job to job by a precarious economy. For many of us, it's a little bit of both.

We tend to distrust organized religion, political parties, the government, corporations, the press, the medical and legal systems, nations, ideologies—pretty much every major institution—and we are averse to associating publicly with any of them. Meanwhile, our media—books, news, entertainment—keeps getting shorter and shorter. And it's not just because we have low attention spans but because we have low commitment spans, too.

But when you look at what we have real affection for—whom we admire, what we respect, and what we remember—it's rarely the institutions and people who come from the Culture of Open Options. It's the master committers we love. In our own lives, we keep swiping through potential partners, but when there's a story online about an elderly couple celebrating their seventieth anniversary, we eat it up. In our own lives, we uproot often, but we line up to get into those famous corner pizza joints and legendary diners that have been around for fifty years. We like our tweets and videos short, yet we also listen to three-hour interview podcasts, binge eight-season fantasy shows, and read long-form articles that comprehensively explain how, say, shipping containers or bird migration works.

You couldn't ask a dozen random young infinite browsers what their most cherished memories are without hearing a few mentions of summer camp. Talk about a counterculture of commitment: Camps are fixed communities imbued with decades of heritage, filled with songs and traditions repeated over and over again, and staffed by a chain of generations between campers and the counselors they eventually become. Even the whole premise of summer camp—that you commit to staying in this place for a few weeks with the same group of people, usually without your phone—is at odds with keeping your options open.

In sports, it's not the one-off moments that are being remembered most these days—it's the epic careers and dynasties. It's Michael Jordan's Bulls, Tom Brady's Patriots, and Michael Phelps's twenty-eight Olympic medals. It's why Serena Williams and Tiger Woods are the most talked-about athletes of the twenty-first century. There's nothing more epic than watching someone grow up and so consistently sustain global excellence in a craft for decades.

As everything dissolves around us, we grasp for anything to hold on to that's more enduring, more meaningful, more hefty than (to borrow a Paul Simon lyric) the "staccato signals of constant information" that fill the digital age. You can see it in the personal DNA kit and genealogy boom, which are driven by our desire to place our lives in a larger historic story. And you can see it in the broader cultural nostalgia boom, in which nineties cover bands, vinyl records, old typewriters, Polaroid cameras, throwback corporate logos and jerseys, and retro fiction, from *Mad Men* to *Stranger Things*, have all blossomed in the past decade. The songwriter Joe Pug asks the right question: "You can call that man history who lives in the past, but can you blame him for asking for something to last?"

At its sweetest and most intimate, we feel this tension in our relationships. We want to go out into the world and have big adventures, but deep down, many of us also dream of just living in the same neighborhood with our best friends. And despite all the dissolution—despite all the preference for novelty over depth, individuality over community, flexibility over purpose—our culture still holds marriage and parenthood as sacred, the last of a dying breed of common commitments.

The tension makes sense. You start missing something as soon as it's mostly gone—and then you hold on to the surviving examples as precious. "As belief shrinks from the world, people find it more necessary than ever that *someone* believe," the nun at the end of Don DeLillo's *White Noise* tells the commitmentless Jack Gladney. "Wild-eyed men in caves. Nuns in black. Monks who do not speak. We are left to believe. Fools, children. Those who have abandoned belief must still believe in us." The historian Marcus Lee Hansen recalled a similar theme in his "principle of third-generation interest": "What the son wishes to forget the grandson wishes to remember." But despite all our love and appreciation for the master committers who remain, many of us still can't make the jump to being committers ourselves. It's our version of the St. Augustine line: "I want to commit, but not just yet."

What accounts for this hesitation? Why do we love committers but act like browsers? I think it's because of three fears. First, we have a *fear of regret*: we worry that if we commit to something, we will later regret having not committed to something else. Second, we have a *fear of association*: we think that if we commit to something, we will be vulnerable to the chaos that that commitment brings to our identity, our reputation, and our sense of control. Third, we have a *fear of missing out*: we feel that if we commit to something, the responsibilities that come with it will prevent us from being everything, everywhere, to everyone.

Because of these fears, the tension sticks around. We act like browsers, we love committers, and we're too scared to make the jump—so we're stuck. That tension, on the individual and collective level, is the point of the departure for this book.

Resolving the tension

But this book is not just about a diagnosis—it also has an affirmative agenda. It's about helping us resolve the tension between browsing and committing—and to do so in a just way. I say "just" because there are forces that are trying to resolve this tension through exclusion or oppression. There are people who tell us to escape the tension by turning back the clock to a time of involuntary commitments. "If only we returned to that glorious age where there were fewer choices about who and what to be," they argue, "then we'll feel good again." And there are other people who aren't looking backward to an ideal past but rather promising an ideal future where all uncertainties will be ironed out—by force, if necessary. This is what we get with cultish zealots of all stripes: an overdose of heavy meaning to combat a meaningless world.

Most of us are rightly skeptical of those who want to turn back the clock to a faux Eden or speed it up to bring about someone else's idea of utopia. But we struggle to put forth a positive alternative to these compelling paths. And as we wait for one to emerge, we are left with the status quo—of Infinite Browsing Mode, of the hallway, of keeping our options open.

But this Culture of Open Options is not a neutral holding pattern. It's a culture that arranges our economy against loyalty to particulars: particular neighborhoods, particular people, particular missions. It's a culture that substitutes a morality of honor—guiding people toward the good and away from the bad—for a morality of indifference. It's a culture that educates for advancement—résumé building and the ladder of success—over attachment: to crafts, causes, and communities of competence.

13

And it's a culture that isn't sustainable. It leads to the abandonment of communities, places, institutions, and reform efforts—and it leaves a vacuum for bad-faith actors to seize. If we, individually and collectively, keep our options open for too long, we're going to be in trouble.

This book proposes a positive alternative to involuntary commitments and the Culture of Open Options. It's a simple and obvious one: *voluntary commitment*. It's the option to choose to dedicate ourselves to particular causes and crafts, places and communities, professions and people. It's not about fully subsuming ourselves in them but about entering into faithful relationships with them. It's not about ironing out all uncertainty but about being willing to temper our doubts enough to have commitments that last a little bit longer, are a little bit stickier, and have a little bit more authority over us. It's not about escaping our liquid world by becoming rigid subjects but rather about transforming our world by becoming solid people.

Some caveats

Some caveats before I continue. For some, this message might already resonate. But for others, I imagine some might be skeptical about one person talking in such sweeping terms about the great tensions of our time. I respect the skepticism, because there are four big risks with talking about something like this.

The first risk is painting with too broad a brush. Nobody can wrap their arms around a whole culture—and the person who tries to is going to say something that isn't true for everyone. All I can say in response is that I'm just one person identifying and attempting to elucidate one pattern that I have noticed about us. Recognizing the pattern has been useful to me. It's given me a lens that has helped me better understand myself and my peers. There's no definitive scientific proof—and all the cherry-picked data in the world isn't going to make this pattern resonate with you if your experience is different.

The second risk of making this argument is that I'm saying something so vague that it's *obviously* true. This is the opposite of the first risk—instead of risking getting something wrong, you risk getting everything right while saying nothing profound. After all, who doesn't like commitment? I hope to avoid this by drawing out the intricate particularities of the phenomenon—the pleasures and pains of Infinite Browsing Mode, the history of our Culture of Open Options, the fears that make up our general fear of commitment, and, most important, the rewards at the other end of long hauls.

The third risk—and, in my opinion, the most significant one— is the risk of talking only to one segment of folks, rather than to everyone. There are people all over the world, as well as people right down the street, who don't have the privilege of keeping their options open. Some people are just hustling for one more option in life. Some people have never found love, never found a place to call home, or never found a stable job. There's a risk of someone reading this and thinking: *What a good problem to have—too many options!*

This is a serious risk. I am just one person—and I have been granted many options in my life. I, myself, bring to this book only my one narrow perspective. But I have taken a few steps to mitigate this risk. First, I tried my best not to write as if the term *young people* means urban, white, and rich young people. And I have worked to bring in other voices to broaden my perspective by interviewing more than fifty long-haul heroes, from all backgrounds, in the process of writing this book.

But I do suggest that struggling with Infinite Browsing Mode is more than a privileged predicament. *Everyone* is facing option overload today. If you're not grappling with it in terms of where to work or which school to go to, you're grappling with it in terms of who to love, where to be, and what to believe. I have a couple of friends who have spent time in state prison, a place where so much is chosen for you. And they have still had to grapple with what type of person they wanted to be while inside: Should they go to this worship service or that one, should they adopt this philosophy or another, should they spend their time this way or that way? This book is for them, too.

One more note on this risk: If you care about advancing the continuing liberation struggles that will give people even more options and free people from even more involuntary commitments, then you need to care about commitment, too. We are only as free as we are today because committed citizens, patriots, builders, stewards, artisans, and companions got us here. And every struggle for justice that remains today will only be advanced if enough dedicated people step up again.

One final risk: Who am I to even talk about this? Let me get this out of the way, loud and clear: I am no where close to being a long-haul hero, myself. I struggle with commitment like other young people today. But I am a commitment superfan—and I have spent the last few years collecting from master committers examples and stories, tips and tricks, reflections and rules of thumb. A poet friend of mine told me that he spent a bit of every day one summer looking at a piece of moss until he really *got* it—and only then did he allow himself to write a poem about it. I guess that's what I've tried to do here: look at commitment for a long time until I understood it, and then, at that point, start writing down what I learned.

The stakes

I wrote this book because I believe whether we resolve this tension—whether more people click out of Infinite Browsing Mode and join up with the Counterculture of Commitment—matters. The stakes are high. On a personal level, they're high because browsing forever can lead to great despair, while dedication can lead to great joy. But the stakes are high on a societal level, too. There are so many big problems to solve, systems to reform, institutions to rebuild, and breaches to repair in the world today. And I believe the biggest barrier to tackling any of these challenges is that there are simply not enough people dedicated to tackling them. There are not enough citizens crusading, patriots celebrating, builders creating, stewards attending, artisans refining, or companions accompanying. Commitment is the first step toward changing the world—and our fears of commitment are standing in the way of jumping in.

Why is commitment necessary to change? Because change happens slow, not fast. Everything that matters takes time—there are no shortcuts. Teaching a student, advancing a cause, healing a divide, rectifying an injustice, revitalizing a town, solving a hard problem, getting a new project off the ground—they all take time. If change happened quickly, we wouldn't need commitment—our initial elation or anger would be enough. But when change takes time, we need something more—something that can get us through the boredom, distraction, exhaustion, and uncertainty that can plague any long-haul effort.

Commitment is also necessary to change because making change often looks less like designing and executing a battle plan and more like cultivating and maintaining a relationship. It is more organic than it is mechanical, more improvised than it is engineered. There are some processes we can't "foolproof," "scale," or "automate." Humans—and human institutions—are too complicated and varied to do so completely. The only way we can change institutions, communities, and people is by entering into relationships with them—by learning their nuances, by building a rapport, by having enough trust and flow to respond nimbly to unexpected circumstances. That's why the best teachers are not the ones who have mastered the textbook—they're the ones who have the deepest relationships with their students. It's why the best mayors are not the smartest but the ones most faithfully committed to their city.

In his final book, Martin Luther King Jr. reflected: "The line of progress is never straight. For a period a movement may follow a straight line and then it encounters obstacles and the path bends. It is like curving around a mountain when you are approaching a city. Often it feels as though you were moving backward, and you lose sight of your goal; but in fact you are moving ahead, and soon you will see the city again, closer by."

Indeed, what is static in successful movements is not the battle plan but the commitment to the movement's vision and values. The sociologist Daniel Bell had a similar insight about belief. He wrote, "Gadgets can be engineered, programs can be designed . . . but belief has an organic quality, and it cannot be called into being by fiat. Once a faith is shattered, it takes a long time to grow again—for its soil is experience." Again, change needs dedicated gardeners, not just clever engineers.

There is an old *Onion* op-ed with the headline: "Somebody Should Do Something About All the Problems." I wrote this book because there is no "somebody" but us. If we cannot become a more dedicated people—if we cannot master, collectively, the slow work of cultivating relationships—"all the problems" will keep piling up. We often assume that some acute and looming threat—be it a foreign invader or a domestic demagogue—will be our civilization's downfall. But if we are to end, that end is just as likely to come from something far less dramatic: *our failure to sustain the work*. It is not only the bomb or the bully that should keep us up at night. It's also the garden untilled and the newcomer unwelcomed, the neighbor unhoused and the stranger unheard, the voice of the public unheeded and the long-simmering calamity unhalted. But we need not be afraid, for we have in our power the ability to perform the slow but necessary work of turning visions into projects, values into practices, and strangers into neighbors. But only if we commit.

Dedicated

Personal joy and communal flourishing would be enough. But there's more: Commitment, I have observed, helps us feel more at peace in existence.

It's hard to be certain about anything these days. We don't know what to believe in, whom to trust, or what will even be around next year. We can't tell what's worth putting time into: what's meaningful and what's a mirage. Some respond to this uncertainty by looking for rigid truths to grasp on to, but for many young people today, myself included, that kind of fundamentalism doesn't work for us. We don't deny that there might be capital-*T* Truth out there. But if there is, we can only see it now, as it is written in Corinthians, "through a glass, darkly." This uncertainty is part of why we have trouble committing. Since we know nothing for sure, we might think it's safer in the hallway. Better not to choose a room at all than to be wrong about the one we choose.

But deep commitments can be a middle way between nihilism and fundamentalism. To commit is to enact partial certainty: to be willing to try something out for a long time, to embody it, and to see what happens. Unlike rigid fundamentalism, which too often involves importing certainty from the outside, commitment is about letting belief grow organically within us. As our own commitment deepens, we slowly develop a clearer understanding of what is good, beautiful, and true. Doubt comes with the territory. But the old spiritual "I Shall Not Be Moved," after all, talks not about a stake driven into the ground but a "tree planted by the water."

It's not only uncertainty that makes us feel off-kilter in existence—it's death, too. The grim fact looms: Our time is limited. For many of us, this is behind our infinite browsing. For some, our fear drives us to endless novelty as we try to play every game at the carnival before closing time. For others, our fear paralyzes, heightening our indecision. The poet Mary Oliver once asked: "Tell me, what is it you plan to do with your one wild and precious life?" I think she meant it as an encouragement, but some of us might find the question haunting: *What if I plan wrong?*

But what I have learned from the long-haul heroes is that these fears fade—at least a bit—as soon we start to commit. I love that the word *dedicate* has two meanings. First, it means to make something holy (like "dedicate a memorial"). But it also means to stick at something for a long time (like "she was dedicated to the project"). I don't think this is a coincidence: We're doing something holy when we choose to commit to something.

At its core, much of commitment is about taking control of our time. Death controls the *length* of our days. But we control the *depth* of our days. Commitment is about choosing to pursue—in the face of our limited length—boundless depth.

Dedicated people aren't in denial about uncertainty or death, but they're more at peace with each. By dedicating their time—by making it holy—they find the antidote to our shared dread. I hope this book can help you join them—to rebel from liquid modernity, become part of the Counterculture of Commitment, and place yourself among the dedicated. There is no better time than now for us to click out of Infinite Browsing Mode, pick a damn movie, and see it all the way through—before we fall asleep.

2

The Pleasures of Infinite Browsing Mode

Before I make the case against keeping our options open, I want to give browsing its due. When I think about the upside of browsing, I think about our late teens and early twenties: a time of liberation defined by moments of freedom from inherited commitments. It's a time when many of us feel like we've escaped a locked room and entered a long hallway, with many different doors to browse.

I've seen all the good that can come from this phase. I've seen people gleefully zip in and out of relationships, in and out of career paths, and in and out of hobbies. There's a shared understanding that everyone will keep things light, *chill*—that there are no hard feelings when someone wants to return to the hallway. I've seen the joy my friends felt when they found a community or identity that was more fitting for their authentic selves—the kid from a long line of doctors learning he wanted to be a comedian; the Orthodox woman who found the space to reject her home community's gender roles; the friends with the long-term partners who discovered they weren't the right fit. And mostly, I've seen all the delight people found in their endless stream of firsts: first cocktail, first salsa dance, first time waking up at someone else's place, first bar scuffle, first midnight horror movie, first time you shared that long-held secret with someone—*first this, first that, first everything.*

Our culture is filled with stories from this phase of life. Perhaps the original browsing mantra is derived from Shakespeare's *The Merry Wives of Windsor*: "The world is your oyster." It's an especially apt phrase for our young adulthood, because the character Pistol coins it in response to an older character saying he will no longer lend him money. "I will not lend thee a penny," Falstaff says, so Pistol responds: "Why, then the world's mine oyster, which I with sword will open." There's also, of course, the romance of hitting the open road. It's the spirit of John Steinbeck's *Travels with Charley*, Willie Nelson's "On the Road Again," and Alfonso Cuarón's *Y Tu Mamá También* (whose one-sentence summary—"Teenagers embark on a road trip and learn a thing or two about life, friendship, love, and each other"—could have been written about dozens of popular films).

Some of our best stories come from the times when we were browsing around trying on new identities without much commitment. There's the dreamy summer romance gone awry. There's that strange gig as a flower deliverer or a roadie for that punk band or a babysitter for that wacky family. There's that month spent in a Santa Fe commune, the season working a lobster boat in Maine, or the night in a dive in Columbus you only half remember. Infinite Browsing Mode is the supreme story generator.

Browsing is *fun*. It gives us room to grow without too much risk, to be more at home in ourselves, and (most fun of all) to have lots and lots of new experiences.

Flexibility

Flexibility—the ability to exit when you don't like something anymore—is the most obvious pleasure of browsing. It means every decision is less consequential, because you can always change your mind and the browsing can continue.

This feeling of lightness is precious when we're young. Often it's simply *a big relief*. By the end of our teenage years, most of us have spent almost two decades inside systems that control most aspects of our lives. Those systems, no matter how good, weigh on us. That's why there's an immense pleasure that comes with the anonymity of going to a new place. You're not burdened by the built-up notions people have *of* you or the built-up expectations people have *for* you.

Even good notions and expectations are heavy. When you're finally anonymous, you might be relieved that you're not expected to be the easygoing one anymore, or the funny one, or the eager helper. This is the joy of the road trip—you can take off at any exit, show up at a bar, and be whoever you want to be. The locals don't need to know you were once a math nerd or prom queen, choirboy or stoner.

These days it's a cliché to be told on a first date: "I have just gotten out of a long-term relationship, and I want to keep this light." For many of us, this is what we want the world to know when we are young: "I just got out of this situation with this one family in this one place with this one role for a very long time—and I'm not going to jump into a whole new one just yet." This is why people who don't "keep it light" in this period of life are often trouble—why it's a red flag when the person down the hall declares you their new best friend on the first day of freshman year or a guy starts talking baby names after a good first date. In *The Unbearable Lightness of Being*, Milan Kundera describes the absence of commitments as causing us "to be lighter than air, to soar into heights, take leave of the earth" and "become only half real," where our movements are "as free as they are insignificant." Some may read this description as derisive, but there's nothing wrong with taking some time when you keep the stakes low. It's helpful, at least for a while.

Flexibility is not just a relief—it's a prerequisite for exploration. If you feel a heaviness in everything—if you're thinking, *If I join this, I can't quit; if I go on this date, we're getting married*—then you limit yourself. And we don't fully know ourselves when we're starting out.

I spent most of my life thinking I wouldn't find a partner. And when I did entertain the thought that I might find one, I had this specific set of ideas worked out about what I thought she would be like. But one summer my friend Jon told me that I was thinking about it all wrong.

"Your partner isn't going to be like a new computer, with detailed specifications," he told me. "Let go of all that and just let your heart figure it out."

Back at school later that year, I tried to lighten up about love. I stopped thinking about it and started feeling about it. And my heart opened up to someone who was nothing like the person I'd pictured. If I wasn't light about the whole experience, it wouldn't have happened. And learning what *doesn't* click for us tells us as much about ourselves as what does. Without that flexibility, there's no exploration—and if there's no exploration, you never get the chance to find out who you are.

Authenticity

The most important fruit of this flexibility, and the exploration that comes with it, is the second pleasure of browsing: the *authenticity* of shedding an inherited commitment that doesn't reflect one's true self.

The Catholic mystic Thomas Merton wrote often about the idea of the "false self"—the "illusory person" who shadows us. The false self is the person who we misguidedly think we want to be—maybe it's the person who we think will best please our family and friends, or gain us acceptance with some in-crowd, or secure our status in our community. But this self, Merton says, is an illusion—it's outside of reality, outside of life, and (for him) outside of God's inner calling for us.

We are unable to see past the illusion, Merton explains, because we "clothe this false self and construct its nothingness into something objectively real." We cover it with "pleasures and glory like bandages" to make it perceptible to ourself and the world, as if it were "an invisible body that could only become visible when something visible covered its surface." You can see examples of this struggle among teenagers—the girl who acts unnecessarily aggressive so that everyone knows she's not to be messed with, the guy who fills his binders with Bible quotes so that everyone knows he's devout, the cocky debater who name-drops Hegel or Nietzsche in casual conversation so that everyone knows he's smart. That's what Merton means by clothing the false self.

But no matter how much wrapping you put on the invisible body, Merton reminds us, your false self is still hollow. Without them, he writes, "there will be nothing left of me but my own nakedness and emptiness and hollowness, to tell me that I am my own mistake." It's not exactly reassuring. But there's a possible happy ending. If we can awaken our authentic self, Merton writes, we can abandon "the vaporous and destructive ego" before it all collapses under its own emptiness. Our youthful browsing can help us shed our false selves. It's a time when we have the space and courage to liberate ourselves from inauthenticity.

During my freshman year of college, there were many people who joined the college versions of whatever they were doing in high school. If they played in the orchestra in high school, they signed up for orchestra; if they were a math whiz, they took many math classes. Then, in the summer after freshman year, there was a wave of quitting. Dozens of people I knew woke up one day, after a little distance, and thought, *I don't really like this very much anymore.* And it was often exactly like Merton's metaphor—these classmates would have T-shirts, trophies, morning routines, and social media identities related to some world they were intimately a part of for a long time. And then one day they would kick it all down and it would crumble in an instant, because their inner experience of these activities had become hollow years before.

Finding authenticity can also take the form of a new calling pushing out an old one. There's the case of falling in love with someone and the fullness of that relationship leading you to question your old identity. Sometimes it's the exact opposite—you find some new sense of meaning in your life, perhaps through a new job, a new religion, or a new political movement—and in the light of your newfound calling, your old relationships feel shallow.

In recent decades, the most prominent example of this shedding of inauthenticity is the process of coming out of the closet. The closet is often experienced in the way Merton described the false self—one speaks and acts a certain way to give the illusion of being straight. Coming out lets all that fall away—and in its place is lightness.

"I realize how stifling the air has been all these years," wrote the writer Merle Miller when he came out in 1971. "I am tired of hiding and I am tired of lying by omission," the actor Elliot Page said when he did the same. The political analyst Steve Kornacki described feeling that "the fear and paranoia are gone"—that his life could "finally make sense" to the people who mattered to him. Liberation, space, openness, relief, wholeness—that's what authenticity feels like.

Even though only some of us experience "coming out," most young people go through a similar process with other parts of their identities—reexamining the past, reflecting on what parts of us are real and which aren't, letting go of inherited commitments that never felt quite right, and taking control of the story we tell the world about ourselves. Toni Morrison puts it well: "You are your own stories and therefore free to imagine and experience what it means to be human." You do not have complete control of your story, but you can "nevertheless create it."

Novelty

The simplest pleasure of browsing is *novelty*—every time we try something new, we experience a rush of excitement. Young people today have experienced more novelty than any other generation in history. It's easier to travel anywhere, learn anything, and meet anyone. And perhaps the biggest development of the last fifty years is that a giant Novelty Machine—the internet—now affords us the ability to connect with the whole world and be fed novelty on demand.

Mark Zuckerberg even once said he believes there is a Moore's law to social network novelty—that sharing will double every year, so that "ten years from now, people will be sharing about one thousand times as many things as they do today." In 2015, he trimmed his sails a bit, writing in a public letter to his newborn daughter that he dreamed of her generation experiencing "100 times more than we do today." As to what experiencing one hundred times more of life looks like, I guess that remains to be seen. But the point has been made: Novelty is the goal.

The idea of soaking in all the novelty you can in life was even given a rallying cry last decade: YOLO, "you only live once." And it came with its own similar-sounding cousin—FOMO, the "fear of missing out" you feel when you are haunted by not living up to the experiential demands of having one life to live. The writer Grady Smith has called the pop music that sprung up around this spirit "#YOLO pop." It emphasizes living for right now, never stopping, and, in the words of the singer Kesha, making "the most of the night like we're gonna die young."

Many people talk about experiencing novelty as "feeling like a kid again." In 2010, the journalist Lu Ann Cahn, pining for the sense of childlike curiosity that wanes when you settle into comfortable routines, set out on a Year of Firsts, committing to do at least one thing she had never done before every day. Over the course of a year, she bought a lottery ticket and rode on a zipline, browsed a comic book store and attended a bodybuilding contest—as well as 361 other firsts. By the end of her Year of Firsts, she felt unstuck—"life opened up in amazing ways," she told a crowd after it was all over. "Firsts"—novelty—are like "fresh air, fresh life." Infinite Browsing Mode, at least for a while, is a real hoot.

3

The Pains of Infinite
Browsing Mode

Eventually, all this fun starts to sour. There comes a point when you're done exploring and you're ready to start digging in. Maybe Willie's "On the Road Again" rings a little less true, and Jason Isbell's "I thought the highway loved me, but she beat me like a drum" starts resonating. Once you've taken advantage of the flexibility, authenticity, and novelty that the hallway has to offer, continuing to browse might leave you feeling paralyzed, isolated, or shallow.

Paralysis

With the flexibility of Infinite Browsing Mode comes the pain of "decision paralysis." The more options you have, and the more times you jump from option to option, the less satisfied you become with any given option—and the less confidence you have in committing to anything. The psychologist Barry Schwartz popularized this idea in his 2004 book *The Paradox of Choice*. Schwartz describes a phenomenon that plagues our everyday lives: the need to choose every detail of everything we consume, from food to clothes to Tupperware. If you've ever gone down a thirty-minute Amazon rabbit hole in search of a new computer keyboard, or scoured Yelp while debating what to eat for lunch, you know what Schwartz is talking about.

A life with no choice, Schwartz explains, would be "almost unbearable." And as our choices start to increase, we get some benefits: more autonomy, more individualization, and more flexibility. But at some point, "choice no longer liberates, but debilitates." That's the paradox: In concept, we seem to always want more choice, but in practice, we often don't.

Examples are everywhere. Take the success of businesses that have prioritized simplicity over large menus of options. The grocery chain Trader Joe's has built a cult following by stripping everything down—selling fewer total items and fewer items per category, all with no brands, no online store, and no promotions. Chipotle did the same by making its menu so short that most customers can list it from memory.

You can see the paradox of choice at work in much more significant situations, too. When I was in college, I was friends with the Mormons on campus. Devout Mormons often feel called to date only fellow Mormons, which meant my friends were choosing from about thirty people in the area instead of thousands like the rest of us. I thought at first that they must feel limited by this, but was surprised to learn that most didn't. Instead, they processed dating differently than their secular friends did. They weren't looking for the absolute perfect match like my other friends, who disqualified potential partners quickly based on surface-level differences. They tended to give each other more of a chance, avoiding the "grass is always greener" trap. They reasoned that relationships mostly work because of a couple's commitment to each other and to a few core values.

Why, Schwartz asks, are we "feeling less and less satisfied even as [our] freedom of choice expands"? One of the easiest explanations is simply shopping exhaustion. All our options lead to what the economist Fred Hirsch called the "tyranny of small decisions"—the thousands of "white, wheat, or rye bread?" moments that eat away at our daily energy, willpower, and working memory. If we were happy with options that are "good enough" to meet our needs, this would be less of a problem. But too many of us, Schwartz explains, are trained to be "maximizers"—unsatisfied until we are "assured that every purchase or decision was the best that could be made."

We're also haunted by unchosen options. If you go get ice cream and order the chocolate, you'll enjoy it. But if you go and consider the chocolate, vanilla, and strawberry and *then* order the chocolate, you enjoy it less, because you're haunted by whether you should have chosen the other two flavors. The more you explore your options, Schwartz explains, the more those "rejected alternatives accumulate." Infinite Browsing Mode breeds ghosts.

And we're not just haunted by actual, real-life alternatives to what we have chosen—we are also haunted by *imagined* alternatives that "combine the attractive features of the ones that do exist." When you decide to move to Chicago, you're not just haunted by what it would be like to live in Miami, DC, or Austin—you're haunted by a mythical city that has Miami's beaches, DC's museums, and Austin's food.

Schwartz's final reason excessive choice paralyzes is that it places excessive responsibility on us. If we *can* curate every aspect of our lives, we become *responsible* for every aspect of our lives. Think about the last time you had to pick a restaurant for a large group. Nobody wants to do it, because no one wants to be responsible for making a suboptimal choice. This is why people flip a coin to make decisions—so they can blame the coin instead of themselves.

What all this adds up to is an across-the-board raising of expectations. If you're going to put in all this time shopping, if you're going to be haunted by all the things you didn't pick, and if you're going to be judged harshly for what you pick—*then what you pick had better be good!* But we can never live up to this standard. Despite all the choice and despite all the Herculean efforts to meet expectations, we end up less satisfied than when we began. The psychologists Donald Campbell and Philip Brickman call it the hedonic treadmill: We are chasing a sense of satisfaction we will never reach—one that fades even further away by our chasing it. Centuries earlier, St. Augustine described the same concept (referencing an ancient tool that required horses to walk in circles all day): "Desire hath no rest, is infinite in itself, endless . . . a perpetual rack, or horse-mill."

My favorite example of this phenomenon in action is a 1998 study by psychologists David Schkade and Daniel Kahneman, entitled "Does Living in California Make People Happy?" The two researchers simply surveyed whether life satisfaction is higher in the Midwest or California. It turns out to be identical. Despite our daydreams, escaping to sunny California—both figuratively and literally—doesn't make us any happier than we are already. Flexibility—the ability to choose differently, to quit everything, to hit the road—is good up to a point, but by itself it's not enough to make us happy. In fact, it can often get in the way.

Anomie

Infinite Browsing Mode can also breed isolation—the malaise of having no connection to anything, of having no expectations set for you. There's a relief that comes from letting go of connections, roles, and even whole communities that forced you to be someone you're not. But after we leave, we're left pining for an alternate community to join. Put another way, being stuck in a locked room is depressing, but so is having to live in the hallway.

In the 1890s, the sociologist Émile Durkheim set out to shed light on the question of why people died of suicide. His investigation is considered one of the first projects of modern social science. No one had so meticulously studied a social phenomenon with modern methods of data collection and observation before. And in studying this specific question, Durkheim was—like the countless sociologists who would eventually emulate him—trying to use a rather narrow topic to discover broader insights about the organization of society.

It was a difficult question to answer, because people die of suicide for various reasons. Was there even a pattern that connected the causes, or was it just random? After gathering evidence—such as the varying suicide rates of different demographic groups, historical time periods, and locations—Durkheim laid out a spectrum that teased out patterns in the randomness. On one side of Durkheim's spectrum are cultures that are heavily integrated and regulated. They are cultures where you feel part of the group, where demands are placed on you for being a member of the group, and where everyone watches out for everybody else—for good (to bring you soup when you're sick) and for ill (to chastise you when you break cultural norms). On the other side of the spectrum are cultures that are only loosely integrated and regulated. They are cultures where you don't really feel like a "member" and where no one is watching out for you—again for good (you can do whatever you want) and for ill (no one cares what happens to you).

What Durkheim discovered was that there are different types of suicide based on people's relationships to these different types of cultures.* One cluster of suicides arise when your individuality is too bound up in the expectations of your culture. You can see it in people dying of suicide because they feel too regulated or too trapped by their culture—people with, in Durkheim's words, "futures pitilessly blocked and passions violently choked by oppressive discipline." This is the case with, for example, the despair of prisoners or non-conformist members of oppressive households or communities.

But on the other side of his spectrum, Durkheim found another cluster of suicides caused by people becoming untethered from community and expectations. Some people despair, he explains, because they know there is a community out there to belong to and yet they don't belong to it. Others despair because they see a lack of community everywhere—and with it, a lack of guidance on what to aspire to, how to act, what to believe in, what to be satisfied with, and how to order one's life. It is the despair of meaninglessness, apathy, and nihilism.

Durkheim calls this type of suicide "anomic suicide"—and the feeling behind it "anomie." It's an apt name—*nomos* is the Greek phrase for "law," and the feeling of anomie is the feeling that there are no standards or laws by which to organize one's life. We have

---

*It should be noted that Durkheim focused solely on cultural—rather than individual and medical—causes of suicide, and wrote before clinical depression and related causes of suicide were better understood.

difficulty making meaning out of life without outside help. "Irrespective of any external regulatory force, our capacity for feeling is in itself an insatiable and bottomless abyss," Durkheim wrote. "But if nothing can restrain this capacity, it can only be a source of torment to itself." Anomie is not the despair of losing a game but the despair of not having a scoreboard—not the despair of being lost on a journey but the despair of having no worthwhile destination.

This, of course, is the academic way to explain anomie. Another way of making the same point is to say you can, in fact, be *too chill*. The writer Alana Massey, in her viral essay "Against Chill," describes the pain of having boyfriends who just wanted to "hang out" in perpetuity—who praised her for not wanting anything serious. The idea of being chill, Massey wrote, "has now slithered into our romantic lives and forced those among us who would like to exchange feelings and accountability to compete in the Blasé Olympics with whomever we are dating."

Massey's account of the downsides of chill are the perfect twenty-first-century explanation of the pains of anomie. To be blasé for too long about relationships is a recipe for unhappiness. Labels aren't handcuffs, Massey quips—they're how people "find the exit during a fire and make sure they're adding vanilla extract to the cake instead of arsenic." And the opposite of chill isn't oppression—it's warmth. We need a bit of that warmth, Massey concludes, to "do something so remarkably unchill as fall in love."

Massey's essay is about romance, but the point applies to other parts of your life. Maybe you've had the experience of someone being too chill about a task, project, community, or job. I think about all the roommate situations I've been in. Most of the time you need your roommates to be chill. But occasionally, that one roommate

you out when you let dirty
when your kitchen is cov-

mmunity. We need people
who we care for and about,
And when authentic com-
cially when it's something

Belonging, the journalist
on returning soldiers feel
they are part of a mission-
ing" society back home,
gs and consumers" like
who describes his time
he was in a community
ar." There was no more
working together on a

ilian life, Junger wrote,
em with individualized
underlying cultural dis-
get some formal psy-
ondition may be some
being bereft of a com-
in facing this kind of
ommunity these days.
day—the idea that is
peech because it reso-
we need to do better

at reaching out to one another, getting to know our neighbors, and coming together.

But anomie is not just about a lack of community. It's also about the lack of regulation—a lack of cultural norms, moral guidance, and rules. And it's not just friends that people are craving. We're also craving the accountability that comes with being part of a mission-driven community. Warm feelings are not enough—we also want expectations to meet, aspirations to seek, and honor to earn.

This is why, counterintuitively, the organizations that ask *more* of their members—the ones that give members big responsibilities rather than solely serving their desires—are thriving. It's why groups that say, "Come whenever you want and do whatever you can, no problem" recruit fewer volunteers than the ones that say, "We need you, we're ready to put you to work, and we are all relying on you." It's why, in school, the teachers and coaches who are the biggest sticklers—the ones who have the highest expectations for their students—often have the most devoted followings. People *want* to be held accountable, because accountability gives us meaning.

In his 1906 speech "The Moral Equivalent of War," the philosopher William James made a similar point. James was part of the generation of Americans who came of age during the Civil War—and whose whole lives, careers, and outlooks were shadowed by the nation's memory of that time. He opens the speech with the striking question of whether anyone his age would trade the experience of the Civil War for an alternative history in which the results of the war were the same—Union triumph, slavery abolished, and so on—but the war itself had never happened.

The answer introduces the puzzle at the center of the speech: Few would take the trade. "Those ancestors, those efforts, those memories and legends" that arose out of the war, James said, were "a sacred spiritual possession worth more than all the blood poured out." And yet, of course, when asked if anyone would have another Civil War, "not one man or woman would vote for the proposition." That's the puzzle: Nobody wants grave struggle, yet when grave struggle is forced upon us and we rise to the occasion, it gives us a precious sense of communal meaning.

To solve the puzzle, James challenges us to develop "moral equivalents of war": collective projects that share the positive qualities of martial valor—projects that necessitate struggle, vigor, fidelity, and courage—while avoiding the negative ones, like division, dehumanization, and bloodshed. If we can set people to work on "the constructive interests" (James suggests, speaking to his specific era, "to freight trains, to fishing fleets in December . . . to road-building and tunnel-making . . .") and see that work as part of valorous, collective struggle, we would "get the childishness knocked out of" us, have "healthier sympathies and soberer ideas," and "tread the earth more proudly."

Of course, James's turn-of-the-century civic romanticism sits a bit uneasy on the other side of the twentieth century, when we saw what can happen when this idea is used for darker ends than fishing in December. But the general point holds: There's a deep part of us that craves authentic community and, with it, something worth fighting for.

Shallowness

My friend once took a thirty-day hiking trip to learn outdoor skills. He and a small group of fellow hikers spent their days somewhat miserably trekking up and down jungle-covered hills in the cold rain. About halfway through the trip, one of the participants left the group due to knee pain. Despite the initial disappointment of having to leave the hike, she was excited to spend her time away doing activities that the rest of the group couldn't do: bungee jumping, taking hot showers, and eating better food than you can cook on a camp stove. But when she returned and they traded memories—her sharing photos from her solo adventures, my friend telling war stories from particularly bad days on the trail—it was obvious that she would have rather stayed with the group. Something pretty special happens when you spend thirty days hiking together, and no amount of bungee jumping can make up for it.

Infinite Browsing Mode comes with a cost: When we spend our time frantically seeking out new experiences, we miss out on the deeper experiences that can only arise from sticking with something for a long time.

Facebook once ran an ad that opens on a young person sitting with her grandmother at dinner. The grandmother is going on and on about something boring, so the grandkid looks down at her phone. The screen erupts with a drummer, a ballet dancer, and a snowball fight all playing out in the room in front of her as she scrolls. The message we're supposed to take away is: With Facebook, you don't have to be in the room with your family; your phone is your ever-present escape hatch.

When we talk about FOMO—the fear of missing out—we're usually talking about missing out on some novel experience, like bungee jumping. Our phones provide a shortcut to those experiences—when you're stuck doing something boring, you at least don't have to miss out on vicariously enjoying something better. But what the grandkid in the ad is really missing out on is the experience of her grandmother's boring story—or maybe the deeper relationship she would have cultivated with her grandma if she committed to engaging with her. What are the real experiences we should worry about missing out on when our grandparents only live once?

By making commitments, we may miss out on the latest novelty. But by *not* making commitments, we will definitely miss out on the deep joy that can only come ten years (or perhaps even ten minutes!) into an experience to which we dedicate our full attention. Sustained engagement is the only way we can bring form to our world—the only way we can separate what is important from what isn't. That's why cultivating the skill of attention is one of the primary goals of education. "The first essential for the child's development is concentration," the educator Maria Montessori wrote. William James called the skill of "voluntarily bringing back a wandering attention, over and over again" the "very root of judgment, character, and will."

Depth usually triumphs over novelty. There's even a name for this principle—the Lindy effect. Named after a longstanding New York deli, the Lindy effect posits that the longer an idea or practice has survived, the longer it will survive into the future. It's why, despite fidget spinners being the talk of the summer of 2017, jump ropes are much more likely to be around in a hundred years, or why the classic old movies we're still watching today are more likely to be watched fifty years from now than this year's blockbuster. If something has managed to last so long already, it will—at least on average—outlast that which hasn't yet proven itself.

Lastingness is—at least for some aspects of life—a rough measure of depth. Most of the time, we can get a sense of how deeply something affected us by whether we remember it years later. All those sporadic tweets you read over the years fade like snowflakes, but that one summer you decided to get really into the samurai and read everything you could on the subject stays with you. All those videos you flicked through are a blur, but that one in-depth documentary you sat down for two hours to watch lingers in your head for years.

None of these observations about the shallowness of novelty are novel. For decades, folks have been warning about the dangers of modern life's superficiality. Unfortunately, most doomsayers are long on diagnosis and short on cure. But there has been one cultural movement in recent decades that has done much to illuminate what the path back to depth could look like.

It all started with a controversial Italian McDonald's in 1986. When the burger chain opened up shop in the Piazza di Spagna, one of the most famous squares in Rome, an outcry erupted across Italy. Thousands rallied to protest what Italians saw as the desecration of a historic center by a symbol of shallow consumerism. One of the chain's opponents, Italian journalist Carlo Petrini, thought signs and angry chants were not enough to convey the depth of the protest's message. So he went to the square and handed out bowls of pasta, a symbol of Italy's deep culinary tradition. With penne in hand, Petrini and his compatriots shouted: "We don't want fast food. We want slow food!"

That day, the international Slow Food movement was born. Taking on the snail as its symbol, it launched with a dreamy "Slow Food Manifesto"—a declaration against "'the fast life' that fractures our customs and assails us even in our homes." Adherents were called to "rediscover the rich varieties and aromas of local cuisines," find "real culture" by "cultivating taste," and defend "slow and prolonged enjoyment."

The Slow Food movement spread around the world. It was perfectly timed for an era when people were beginning to notice the downsides of the global forces that had been prioritizing quantity over quality, spectacle over depth, the abstract and universal over the particular and local—and, of course, the fast over the slow. It felt bigger than food: It was a whole different mindset, and offered a whole different ethos, than that being served up by the global corporations of the day.

Thirty years later, a wave of "Slow" movements have spread to dozens of other areas of life. Architect John Brown has proposed Slow Home—an antidote to cheap and easy suburban sprawl. Psychologist David Tresemer has proposed Slow Counseling—an antidote to "one pill fits all" therapies. Susan Clark and Woden Teachout have proposed Slow Democracy—the local, community-based form of politics that runs counter to the spectatorial mass politics of cable news debate shows and presidential campaign ads. There's even Slow Gaming—a call for video games that are more humane, more reflective, and more personal.

Speed and shallowness are often linked. Zygmunt Bauman liked to quote the Ralph Waldo Emerson line: "In skating over thin ice, our safety is in our speed." When there's not much underneath the surface of our superficial routines, best to move fast—from novelty to novelty—to distract ourselves from our shallowness. When we force ourselves to move slow again, as the Slow movement calls us to do, we confront it. The confrontation can be terrifying. But as we move through it, we can begin to rediscover depth.

We want the flexibility, the authenticity, and the novelty of browsing. But we don't want the paralysis, the anomie, or the shallowness that comes with them. We like unlimited choice, but we also like Trader Joe's. We want to be liberated from inauthentic commitments, but we also want moral equivalents of war. We want the Novelty Machine to share something interesting with us every day, but we also want deep conversation with old friends over slow food.

Aristotle taught that building virtue was the art of balancing extremes. Courage strikes a balance between being cowardly and being reckless. Wit strikes a balance between being boring and being buffoonish. Friendliness strikes a balance between being quarrelsome and being fawning. We all wonder what the right balance is. Where can we find flexibility without paralysis, authenticity without anomie, novelty without shallowness?

This is part of why the Counterculture of Commitment is so intriguing. Long-haul heroes seem to have struck the right balance. They seem to have found another way—not the locked room, not the hallway, but the room that one freely chooses. By settling in for a while, the dedicated have found a resolution to the tension that torments the rest of us.

4

Between Liberation
and Dedication

You may be wondering: Isn't this tension what every young adult feels, across all times and places? Yes, but I believe we are *especially* stuck in Infinite Browsing Mode today because our society has relatively recently experienced an explosion of new options. For the average American, the increase in options during the twentieth century—in the number of available opportunities, choices, novel experiences, and ways of life—is hard to overstate.

A century or two ago, most parts of most peoples' lives were completely encumbered by involuntary, inherited commitments. For many, it was because of technological necessity—you had to stick with your family and community to survive. Sunlight and seasons structured the days and years. The number of people you met in your lifetime—and the variety of ways of life you saw—was limited. So much was chosen *for* you.

Political and religious systems enforced other involuntary

commitments. The law structured most of a woman's economic and social life around her relationship to her father and her husband. If you were not white, you likely were born in a segregated hospital, educated in an underfunded school, and forced into particular jobs and particular neighborhoods. If you were disabled, your community had low expectations for what you could do with your life. If you were gay, you had to hide parts of yourself. If you were different in any way—if you were a guy with longer hair, a Muslim or an atheist, a musician who wanted to sing differently, a family who wanted to live differently, or a person who just wanted to build their life around some alternative culture—there were fewer publicly acceptable lives available to you. For so long, so many were tied to their hometowns, their parents' wishes, their inherited religions and trades, and their high school sweethearts. For most people, the idea of "keeping your options open" was alien, because there were so few options to begin with.

But a series of liberatory struggles and developments in the twentieth century untied many of these involuntary commitments. Thanks to new technology and the work of justice movements, unchosen attachments to places, roles, lifestyles, and expectations have loosened. For many more people in many more ways, options abound.

This is not to suggest that these liberatory shifts are complete—the past century's justice movements, in particular, are continual works in progress. Rather, it is to point out that the big story most of us are swimming in is the story of liberation from involuntary commitments.

Our culture celebrates this ethic of liberation. The plot of every other movie seems to revolve around a protagonist who, having been involuntarily committed to something, manages to liberate him- or herself to be something different. The poor orphan Luke Skywalker wants a bigger life than the one he is condemned to on Tatooine. Elle Woods could never work in the law, it is assumed—until she defies that prejudice and proves that she can. Jack and Rose on the *Titanic*, Aladdin and Jasmine of Agrabah—they are not supposed to fall in love, but they break free anyway.

In the film *Billy Elliot*, an eleven-year-old coal miner's son dreams of leaving town to dance ballet. At the beginning of the movie, his father is appalled—he has expectations for who, what, and where Billy's going to be. But Billy's dreams prove bigger than these expectations. By the film's end, he is freed from his fate and goes off to ballet school. It's a textbook example of our age's beautiful story: the story of liberation.

Stuck in the middle

But liberation isn't enough. We need to be freed from involuntary commitments, but that freedom isn't sufficient for a fulfilling life. The car lets us go anywhere, the internet lets us see anything—but happiness has not come automatically. If Jack and Rose had survived their love affair, they would still have questions about how to feel or what to do after that initial spark faded. Romance movies usually end in death or a wedding day—we rarely see the actual marriage.

The same goes for dramatic moments of finding authenticity. After you tell people who you really are—after that brave day when you make your true self known—*well, then what?* What happens when Billy Elliot starts finding ballet school to be tedious or exhausting? What happens when he starts to wonder if he should have been a dentist or a carpenter—or when he has to balance his career teaching ballet with spending time with his children?

Liberation isn't enough for us collectively, either. Despite all the liberatory tools available to us—despite our ability to think freely, to see through the lies of false objectivity, to find all the cracks in the stories we have been told—the world we want to live in has not automatically emerged from the ashes of the old one. The liberatory spirit of our age has helped us tear down bad institutions, but it hasn't helped build up new ones. It has helped avoid some tragedies, but it hasn't built global peace. It has helped diagnose the maladies of our time, but it hasn't figured out a cure.

Even the task of advancing liberation itself—planning the next justice campaign, building the next coalition, organizing the next action—requires more than the tools of liberation. Critique, skepticism, and analysis are not enough—a free world requires creativity, belief, unity, and inspiration, too. "Where there is no vision," it says in Proverbs, "the people perish." That's because liberation is only half of the story of who we are. The other half is *dedication*. People want to be free, but we want to be free to then *do* something.

You can find this liberation-dedication cycle everywhere. It's built into the marriage ceremony—you separate from your families and join together to make another. This is also what you see when people change beliefs: desecration and then reconsecration. You might become alienated from an old community, lose faith in it, and detach, perhaps with the help of some sacrilegiousness—the profane jokes and critical comments that loosen a system's grip on you. But then you develop faith in a new community, and attach again, often with ceremonies of rehallowing—setting aside a part of your life where you can find the sacred again.

This cycle was key to the ancient practice of alchemy. Though it's mostly remembered today as an odd form of proto-chemistry, alchemy's practitioners experienced it as a rich mythic system meant to aid in personal spiritual transformation. The alchemical process of "turning lead into gold" was an elaborate metaphor for a spiritual process: raising up leaden human souls into sanctified, "golden" ones.

The material process of alchemy consists of three stages. The first, the *nigredo*, or black stage, involves stripping, breaking, and dissolving down the lead. In the second stage, the *albedo*, or white stage, the dissolved lead is washed and purified. In the third stage, the *rubedo*, or red stage, the material is placed into fire to solidify into a new form. At the end of the process emerges gold: light made solid.

For alchemists, this was how to become a full individual—liberating yourself from the dead weight of inherited routine *and* dedicating yourself to new, more life-affirming beliefs and meanings. The hard news is that both sides of this process—cleaving and leaving, separation and synthesis, dissolving and solidifying—are not automatic. You need to learn how to liberate yourself *and* how to dedicate yourself.

Dedication requires the cultivation of what could be called the "dedicatory virtues." It requires *imagination*—the ability to envision what isn't there just yet. It requires *synthesis*—the ability to make connections. *Focus* (the ability to concentrate) and *doggedness* (so you can return to the same task again and again, even if there's nothing new about it) are key. So is *passion*—the enthusiasm required to sustain engagement. And there can be no passion without *reverence*—the ability to be awed by something. Above all, dedication requires *commitment*—the ability to stick with something, despite there being other available options.

It's hard to make a movie about dedication. The film *Whiplash*, for example, is the inverse of *Billy Elliott*. It starts on a kid's first day as a drummer in a new jazz ensemble. It has no scene of the kid's dad telling him not to drum; no scene where the kid sneaks away to forbidden drum lessons in the dead of night; no dramatic speech that culminates in the kid shouting, "I don't want to be an accountant, I want to drum!" It's just two hours of a kid having a hard time learning how to drum—of trying and failing, again and again, to stay on pace with his drumming heroes. It's also not that pleasant to watch, which is probably why there are many more movies like *Billy Elliot* than like *Whiplash*.

Knowing much about how to liberate ourselves and not that much about how to dedicate ourselves has left us stuck in liberation-dedication purgatory. We've been freed from many involuntary commitments, but we struggle to make voluntary ones. We leave, but we don't cleave. We desecrate, but we don't consecrate. We melt down, but we don't solidify into something else.

Liquid modernity

The result of this predicament—of our ability to melt things down without making them solid again—is what Zygmunt Bauman was referring to when he coined the term *liquid modernity*. Modernity, to Bauman, was defined by the process of melting down traditional "solids." Things like old loyalties, irrelevant obligations, hereditary estates, familial shackles—"the dense tissue of ethical obligations"— were melted away.

But these traditions were melted down, Bauman notes, with the intention of replacing them with something else. And that's what happened, at first. We replaced traditional communities with constitutions, nation-states, bureaucracies, corporations, militaries, factories, and heavy machinery. Everything was big: To be a powerful company meant having a big factory; to be a powerful state meant having a big military; and to be a powerful city meant having big bridges and railway stations. Individuals could find their way by joining up with one of these large, lasting enterprises. And these institutions' time horizons were long: If you joined an enterprise at a young age, you could expect it to be there when you retired.

But in the second half of the twentieth century, Bauman argues, something changed. The melting down became an end in itself. Change became the only permanence, and uncertainty the only certainty. It wasn't factory owners who earned the most money now—it was the controllers of flexible information, energy, and financial networks. Power used to come from durability—bulky, secure, lasting enterprises. But in this new, "liquid" modernity, power came from flexibility—the ability to become a new form amid all the change. For corporations, the goal was no longer making investments today to assert control over the future, but rather releasing attachments today to ensure they could transform in the future. Enterprises started building projects using a flurry of short-term contracts, rather than by building up a stable labor force. You would no longer, Bauman wrote, "plant a citrus-tree grove to squeeze a lemon"—you would make a short-term deal for the lemon and call it a day.

In this new form of modernity, everything—both the people and the structures—became like Proteus, the Greek sea god who could assume whatever shape he pleased. Thus, the central metaphor of *liquid* modernity: To be liquid is to be unable to hold your shape. This is what happens when you're caught between liberation and dedication: You are melted down, and you can't find a way to become solid again.

You can see liquid modernity in action all around us. How we work, how we date, how we consume, how we move, and how we act as citizens have all been changed by this great loosening.

For every non-millennial who changed jobs in 2019, three millennials did. One recent Deloitte study found that four in ten millennials envision leaving their job within two years. And this trend isn't about being young—it's a generational shift. Over the last two decades, the number of places people worked in the first five years after graduating college has risen from 1.6 for those graduating between 1986 and 1990 to 2.85 for those graduating between 2006 and 2010.

Some of us are voluntarily job-hopping, but most of us have been forced into instability by mass layoffs and the gig-ification of the workforce. There are an estimated 55 million workers in what has come to be called "the precarious economy": freelancers, day laborers, temp workers, subcontractors, and gig workers, such as Uber drivers or TaskRabbits. Even if many of these precarious workers *wanted* to commit to some line of work, the structure of the economy is preventing them from doing so.

There's been a loosening in relationships, too. In 1962, three in five Americans under thirty were married. Fifty years later, that's plummeted to just one in five. But millennials aren't choosing promiscuity over marriage. A San Diego State University study found that millennials have fewer sexual partners than baby boomers or Gen Xers did when they were young. Instead, young people are likely delaying marriage in part because they are exposed to way more people—and with that, way more potential partners—than their parents were. We are paralyzed by indecision, always wondering whether a better partner is just around the corner. Dating apps such as Tinder, which have turned maximizing exposure to potential partners into a science, don't help. "The hardest part," as podcast host PJ Vogt once put it, "is seeing all the people who seem pretty good."

Many young people are also scarred by memories of divorce and family dissolution, and they want to be certain they won't face the same fate. There's also been a decline in what you could call attachment entities: the clubs, churches, and work communities where you are given a chance to get to know another person beyond surface-level qualities. On top of all this, of course, widespread economic insecurity doesn't exactly help people settle down.

Meanwhile, many young people have embraced the so-called sharing economy, where more goods—from cars to bikes to clothes to even home-cooked meals—are being repackaged from something we own or make to something we rent as a service or buy prepackaged. But "sharing economy" isn't really the right name for it. A sharing economy implies a culture of sharing—a community that feels reciprocal obligations to one another. The researchers Giana M. Eckhardt and Fleura Bardhi have a better term: the *access economy*. It's an economy where without committing to anything, you can (if you're wealthy enough to afford it) access everything. Instead of investing in office space, you can get a coworking-space subscription. Instead of buying full albums, you can listen to individual songs with Spotify. Instead of planning meals and shopping for them, you can get the recipes and ingredients delivered to your door.

This last development in particular is a revealing test case. The preparation and consumption of meals has historically been one of the major venues of ownership, identity, and community. How we shopped, preserved ingredients, cooked, plated, served, enjoyed, recycled, and grew our food has long been a source of our personal pride. But in recent years, we've undergone a transformation. Ads for subscription meal kits are everywhere. Fast casual chains are booming. "Ghost restaurants"—restaurants that only exist to serve deliveries—are popping up in cities across America. And according to recent surveys by the Food Marketing Institute, almost half of all meals eaten by American adults are eaten alone.

Thanks in large part to professional instability, soaring rents, and the increased financial difficulty of buying a home, many young people are bouncing from neighborhood to neighborhood and city to city. All this moving makes us feel less connected to the communities we live in. Two-thirds of young people report not feeling connected with our communities—and half of us say that we do not have time to participate locally. We trust our neighbors less than any other generation—and when asked in one survey if we had ever taken ten "neighborly actions" (such as smiling at neighbors, learning neighbors' names, or entering neighbors' homes), we scored much lower than our older counterparts.

The result of all this is a whole lot of loneliness. Three in ten young people report feeling lonely often, and one in five report having no friends at all. Friendship and the institutions that cultivate and maintain friendships, of course, require commitment.

In the past half century, net confidence in almost every American institution has declined. Surveys find we trust the government, the president, and Congress less than we did before. We trust the press and the media less. We trust the medical, legal, and education systems less. And we trust religion and corporations less. Half of all

Americans believe the "overall system" has failed them. And that's just the state of institutional trust when you poll Americans of all ages. When you poll only young people, the numbers are even lower. Fewer than three in ten young people have "a lot of confidence in" banks, the justice system, Silicon Valley, mayors, governors, the federal government, and the news media.

As a result, we are affiliating much less with larger institutions and identities than our grandparents did. Whereas almost two-thirds of Americans over sixty-five belong to a religious congregation, only four in ten Americans under thirty do. Though the generations report similar levels of "sense of wonder about the universe" or "thinking about the meaning and purpose of life," almost twice as many members of the youngest generation report being "spiritual but not religious" as their elder counterparts. And while about half of young Americans describe themselves as political independents, a substantial share of self-described independents consistently vote for one party over another—indicating that these folks aren't actually *ideologically* independent but rather have an aversion to committing to a label.

I could go on, but you get the point: Our bonds have loosened, our trust has thinned, and "keep your options open" has become our generational motto. Bauman was onto something: We are liquid people in a liquid world. Caught between liberation and dedication, we are glad to not be rigid, and yet we pine for a more solid life amid the dizzying flow.

No going back, no staying here

The tension between browsing and committing plays out on an individual level, haunting the pleasures of flexibility, authenticity, and novelty with the pains of paralysis, anomie, and shallowness. And it plays out on the collective level, too, trapping us in liquid modernity. Some describe this tension as latent anxiety or burnout or a general sense of disquiet. Some call it our collective malaise or widespread unraveling or mass alienation. Some see it as simple impotence—the feeling of wanting to do something but being unable to do it. Something's off. But what do we do about it?

Some answer this question by saying we should go back to involuntary commitments. You could go through all the liberatory developments and struggles of the past century and find groups devoted to turning back the clock. Some people pine for a return to rigid hierarchies. Others cling to old institutions—playacting the supposed glory days before people lost trust. Still others pretend that their common sense is universal, their judgments "neutral and objective," and their personal vision of society "perfectly natural and necessary." There are even folks who have given up on cars and the internet to go live in the woods.

Sometimes "going back to certainty"—to involuntary commitments—isn't even about going back. You can "go forward to certainty," too. The poet W. H. Auden wrote about the two kinds of people who dreamed of "the Happy Place where suffering and evil are unknown"—the Arcadians and the Utopians. The Arcadians are "turn back the clock" types. They dream of an Eden—an Arcadia—where "the contradictions of the present world have not yet arisen." In Arcadia, no one needs to speak of commitment, because everyone fits so snugly in their way of being that they are not even self-conscious about being that way. The Utopians want the opposite. They dream of a "New Jerusalem," where the contradictions of the present world "have at last been resolved." In Utopia, no one needs to talk of commitment, because everyone is so committed to and satisfied with their role in the new order that they don't even have to think about it.

But we can't—and shouldn't—go back, or forward, to certainty. As the writer Michael Weiss points out, the Arcadians tend to leave out all the suffering they would have to ignore to live peacefully in their own private Edens. They may not cause human suffering, but their indifference exacerbates it. What becomes of a person who chooses "art and beauty" over "living human beings"? It's easy for people who fit snugly in an old world to pine for it. But for those who did not—who were oppressed or hemmed in by it—this type of nostalgia is disturbing.

As for the Utopians, there is no utopia in which we all fit snugly. A defining feature of humanity, the philosopher Roberto Unger wrote, is that we "overflow our contexts"—that there is more inside us, individually and collectively, than could ever be contained by any possible social arrangement. Immanuel Kant put the impossibility of perfect order well, too: "Out of the crooked timber of humanity, no straight thing was ever made." And, as Weiss notes, Utopians tend to leave out what needs to be done to force everyone into their vision of perfection. Many "would happily wade through rivers of blood to reach their New Jerusalem."

So we're still here in liberation-dedication limbo. Going back to involuntary commitments—being stuck behind a locked door—is not tenable. It doesn't fit with who we are: We need to have some flexibility, find our authentic selves, and experience some novelty. But living in the hallway isn't tenable, either: We want more than paralysis, anomie, and shallowness. And if we remain stuck between liberation and dedication for much longer, there might not even be a world left to dedicate ourselves to when we get around to it. It's like the old bartender line at closing time: "You don't have to go home, but you can't stay here."

II.

THE COUNTERCULTURE
OF COMMITMENT

5

Long-Haul Heroism

On New Year's 1863, at midnight, the Emancipation Proclamation would take effect. This moment was monumental—the formal culmination of a centuries-long struggle against American slavery. To celebrate, thousands of abolitionists gathered at the Boston Music Hall.

The poets Henry Wadsworth Longfellow and Ralph Waldo Emerson helped organize the event. Twenty years before, Longfellow had published "Poems on Slavery" to help support the abolitionist cause—and had spent the following two decades sponsoring abolitionist events and organizations, funding enslaved people seeking freedom, and working to support Senator Charles Sumner's legislative efforts to end slavery. Emerson had started lecturing against slavery nineteen years before. He used the magazine he had cofounded, the *Atlantic*, to advance the cause, and even welcomed the abolitionist militant John Brown into his Concord home.

That night, when the crowd noticed Harriet Beecher Stowe in the gallery, they started waving their handkerchiefs and chanting, "*Mrs. Stowe! Mrs. Stowe! Mrs. Stowe!*" With her face (as one report observed) "all aglow with pleasure and excitement," Stowe moved toward the rail, bowed, and wiped tears away from her eyes as the crowd erupted. A decade or so earlier, after she lost her eighteen-month-old son to cholera, Stowe was inspired to write *Uncle Tom's Cabin*. It would become the most influential text of the abolitionist cause.

William Lloyd Garrison, the abolitionist newspaperman, was also in the gallery. Thirty-two years earlier, he had launched the *Liberator*, a weekly paper that served as a community bulletin board for the movement. His first issue stated his mission loud and clear: "I will not equivocate—I will not excuse—I will not retreat a single inch—AND I WILL BE HEARD." And he was: By the 1860s, you could find *The Liberator* in statehouses, governors' mansions, Congressional offices, and eventually the White House. During his tenure as editor, Garrison was attacked by mobs, indicted in various states, and shunned by polite society.

But in the Boston Music Hall that day, celebration was in the air. Emerson read a poem written for the occasion. A full choir sang Mendelssohn's "Hymn of Praise" and Handel's "Hallelujah Chorus." Down the block, at the Tremont Temple Baptist Church, William Cooper Nell presided over another celebration, proclaiming: "From the Atlantic to the Pacific, there shall not be found a tyrant to wield the lash, nor a slave to wear the chain." Almost four decades earlier, his father had helped found the Massachusetts General Colored Association. Two decades later, Nell followed in his father's footsteps, helping found the New England Freedom Association to aid refugee slaves and resist the Fugitive Slave Act. The Reverend Charles

Bennett Ray was in the church, too. He had become involved in the cause thirty years earlier as a promoter of the Underground Railroad and editor of another abolitionist newspaper, the *Colored American*.

The final speaker of the night was Frederick Douglass. Twenty-four years earlier, he had escaped from slavery himself. In the subsequent decades, he would become a world-renowned preacher; a leader at various abolitionist conferences; a writer at the *Liberator*; a founder of his own newspaper, the *North Star*; an author of a best-selling memoir about his time enslaved; and a lobbyist of various politicians, including President Abraham Lincoln. In his speech that night, punctuated by jubilant shouts of "Amen!" and "Bless the Lord!" he said that the nation's "period of darkness" had come into a "dawn of light."

People ran back and forth from the telegraph office to get word if the proclamation had indeed been issued. "Eight, nine, ten o'clock came and went," Douglass reported later, "and still no word." Some worried Lincoln had gone back on his promise. But then someone ran in, shouting: "It is coming! It is on the wires!" Not long after, it was read aloud: "I do order and declare that all persons held as slaves . . . henceforward shall be free."

The crowd exploded in what Douglass would later describe as a "wild and grand" scene. People threw hats and bonnets in the air. Old nemeses from intramovement divides hugged. Douglass's friend began singing his favorite hymn, and the crowd joined him: "Sound the loud timbrel o'er Egypt's dark sea, Jehovah hath triumphed, his people are free!" When they were kicked out of the hall at midnight, the crowd walked to Twelfth Baptist Church—a church that had been called "the Fugitive Slave Church" because it was a longtime hub of the Underground Railroad in Boston. They celebrated until dawn. These abolitionists' decades of work had paid off. They had won a victory for humanity.

We often hear that "it is what it is"—that nothing ever changes, and there's nothing we can do about it. That's wrong. What happened in Boston on New Year's 1863 shows that when you commit to something—when you push at it over the course of many years; when you give your varied talents to it; when you fight off the distraction, uncertainty, and exhaustion that threaten your will to keep going—you sometimes win. There's no reason not to think that if we, too, dedicate ourselves to the callings of *our* time—if we work to become long-haul heroes as well—similar celebrations of long-hoped-for triumph await us, as well.

Hollywood dragon-slaying

Most of us feel drawn to commit to something bigger than ourselves. It's the romantic vision of youth: To be a hero, standing for a cause; to "make something of ourselves;" to leave behind the humdrum routines of certainty and go in search of noble adventure. This impulse can guide us to a third way between Infinite Browsing Mode and involuntary commitments. It's the path of *voluntary commitment*: of choosing a room off the hallway, of dedicating oneself after liberating oneself, of committing after browsing.

But too often, we associate this kind of commitment with big, brave moments. Hollywood challenges us to prove our dedication through cinematic dragon-slaying. And despite the popular notion that young people are self-centered, I actually think we are ready to fight for something bigger than ourselves—as long as the dragon we need to fight appears in some singular form at some singular time. If the invader comes into our house, we are ready to defend our family. If the bigot shows up at our store, we are ready to call them out. When the epic march against all the problems is announced, we are ready to join in.

Maybe you've seen the popular ABC show *What Would You Do?* with John Quiñones. Hidden cameras are set up in some deli, restaurant, or street corner, and actors play out some morally fraught scene in order to test the responses of unsuspecting bystanders. Sometimes the actors play an underaged kid asking for you to buy them alcohol or cigarettes. Sometimes they play a racist waitress. Sometimes they play a hungry family short on cash at a grocery store checkout line. As you watch the bystanders grapple with whether to intervene, you ponder the question: If presented with a similar situation, "What would I do?"

This is what I mean by Hollywood dragon-slaying—it's "what would you do" heroism. You enact your voluntary commitments by acting on singular moments when your commitments come into play. It's like the Shakespeare line: "Some are born great, some achieve greatness, and some have greatness thrust upon 'em." That last option is what we are ready for: Show us the dragon, and we'll slay it.

But here's the problem with Hollywood dragon-slaying: In reality, when the cinematic moments arrive, they don't really move the needle much. The epic speeches given at the perfect times don't actually shift opinion. The big rallies—and the big takedowns—don't help much, either. The dramatic scene where you sit down with a troubled child and tell him that he's allowed to cry (while string music plays in your head) doesn't solve that kid's problems. Throwing the bad guy in jail doesn't heal the community. And playing a romantic song in the rain doesn't lock in the relationship.

If all it takes is standing up among like-minded people and shouting "Mr. President, sir, I reject you!" and taking in the applause, we would all be knights and valor wouldn't be worth much at all. This is what you discover about Twitter after a while—it's just a machine that lets you slay dragons every hour and, in making it so easy, shows how fruitless the whole endeavor is. Hollywood dragon-slaying comes cheap.

The real dragon-slayers

Real change does not look like Hollywood dragon-slaying, because real change takes a long time. Creating relationships takes a long time—and healing broken relationships does, too. Forming communities—turning strangers into neighbors and spaces into places—takes a long time, and so does healing community divisions. Building institutions takes a long time, and reviving institutions that have been corrupted does, too. There is no perfect blueprint you can use to swiftly engineer the results you want. The process is slow and organic, not quick and mechanical.

Political change takes an especially long time. As Max Weber described it, "politics is a strong and slow boring of hard boards." To take ideas from "unthinkable" to "thinkable but fringe" to "debatable" to "popular" to "consensus" is a trek. Remember that old mantra: "First they ignore you, then they laugh at you, then they fight you, then you win." Each of those phases lasts a while.

And the real dragons standing in the way of these goals—of making and sustaining these relationships with particular ideas, people, crafts, and communities—are nothing like the dragons you see in movies. They're much more wily and terrifying. The real dragons are, to start with, the fears that stop us from making these commitments in the first place. They're: *the fear of regret*—that if we commit to something, we will later regret having not committed to something else; *the fear of association*—that if we commit to something, we will be vulnerable to the chaos that that commitment brings to our identity, our reputation, and our sense of control; and *the fear of missing out*—that if we commit to something, the responsibilities that come with it will prevent us from being everything, everywhere, with everyone.

And it's not just the fears of making commitments that stand in our way—it's the threats to sustaining them, too. These real dragons look a lot less like some cartoonish evildoer and a lot more like the everyday boredom, distraction, and uncertainty that can erode our ability to commit to anything for the long haul.

If these are the real dragons, the real dragon-slayers are those who have made a difference over a long period of time. They're the long-haul heroes who have overcome their fears of, and beaten back the threats to, sustained commitment. Their commitments might culminate in a big moment, like the Emancipation Proclamation, but only as a result of thousands of little ones. The reformer Jacob Riis described it this way: "Look at a stone cutter hammering away at his rock, perhaps a hundred times without as much as a crack showing in it. Yet at the hundred-and-first blow it will split in two, and I know it was not the last blow that did it, but all that had gone before."

The folk singer Pete Seeger talked about it as a seesaw. One side is planted firmly on the ground, weighed down by boulders. The side in the air has an empty basket atop it. A small group of people patiently work to fill the basket with sand, one teaspoon at a time. The crowd watching scoffs, because nothing is changing. But one day, the whole seesaw is going to flip—not little by little, but all at once. People will ask, "How did it happen so suddenly?" The answer, of course, is all those teaspoons over the years.

Long-haul history

History is filled with dedicated people who refused to believe that nothing ever changes—but who nevertheless understood that change takes a long time. There's the Hungarian physician Ignaz Semmelweis, who spent two decades popularizing the discovery that handwashing fights the spread of disease. He went from being ignored, dismissed, harassed, and called an extremist for his sustained insistence on his discovery to being one of the public health icons of the century. Today, a university, hospital, coin, and even a planet bear his name.

Think of President Jimmy Carter and the Guinea worm. Carter spent the first fifty years of his life aspiring to higher office—and in November 1980, with his failed presidential reelection bid, it all came crashing down. He could have retired, cashed in on his fame, and become cynical about public life. Instead, he committed to taking the long road on a few simple causes. One was eradicating Guinea worm disease, which—when Carter started working on it—afflicted 3.5 million people per year, caused immense suffering, and exacerbated global poverty. It wasn't a flashy cause, and it would not gain immediate headlines, but the disease was horrible and the fix was attainable. Today, thanks to the work of the Carter Center, there are fewer than fifty cases annually in humans. When asked about his hopes in his old age, Carter—who's now in his nineties—is known to reply: "I'd like for the last Guinea worm to die before I do."

Or consider the suffragists' long haul. In July 1848, New York teenager Charlotte Woodward Pierce traveled by wagon with six friends to the Seneca Falls Convention, the first major American women's rights convention ever held. The most hotly contested topic at the convention was whether the group should advocate for voting rights for women. Think about that: This was a gathering of the most radically fringe feminists in the country, and the idea of women voting was controversial even among *them*! Yet the attendees, including Pierce, came out of that convention committed to walking the long road together to suffrage. Seventy-two years—and dozens of organizations, hundreds of books and newspapers, thousands of campaigns, tens of thousands of marches, hundreds of thousands of letters, and millions of persuasive conversations—later, the once-unthinkable idea had become law. By the time the Nineteenth Amendment had been ratified, all of Pierce's fellow signatories to the convention's Declaration of Sentiments had died. Pierce was the only one to live long enough to see the culmination of her and her comrades' commitment. Change takes time, but it happens.

Focus in on any locale, and you'll find long-haul heroes who helped build it. Nina Otero-Warren spent the 1920s as the superintendent of public schools for Santa Fe County, New Mexico—and devoted her time in office to improving education for rural, Hispanic, and Native students. She repaired run-down buildings, raised teacher's salaries, started a high school and adult learning program, and pressured the federal government for more funding for Native education. She negotiated the transformation of Santa Fe's schools into tri-cultural institutions, incorporating Native and Spanish arts, crafts, literature, and practices into local curricula. She joined boards and women's organizations, brokered compromises between various Santa Fe interests and factions, and preserved historic structures in Santa Fe and Taos. She even wrote in a national magazine about the beauty of the Southwest to help inform the nation about the glory of her region's culture and environment. There was no cinematic moment in Otero-Warren's life that captures the imagination—just decades of work improving her community. And there are tens of thousands of Otero-Warrens in every corner of our country's history.

The rest of the Black Freedom Struggle, beyond abolition, is a series of long hauls. After one of her friends was lynched in the spring of 1892, Ida B. Wells began systematically investigating lynchings. That fall, she published a pamphlet: *Southern Horrors: Lynch Law in All Its Phases*. After its publication, Wells went on lecture tours around Britain and America to gain allies. During the tour, she kept investigating lynchings to deepen her argument. That work culminated in the 1895 book *A Red Record: Tabulated Statistics and Alleged Causes of Lynchings in the United States*, one of America's first examples of modern data journalism. Throughout the campaign, she worked to persuade Northern and foreign investors that lynchings were anarchic threats to economic development, encouraging them to avoid the risks by boycotting the South until anti-lynching legislation passed.

Wells not only protested opponents—she pressured allies, too. She aggressively pushed the newly formed NAACP to make anti-lynching laws a policy priority—and when the organization didn't take sufficient action, she distanced herself from it. In the late 1920s, she tired of having to lobby government officials from the outside, so she ran for Illinois state senate herself. When she got too old to organize as fiercely, she threw herself into writing a useful autobiography to teach young people about the struggle.

Twenty-five years after her first pamphlet, Congress began debating anti-lynching legislation—and three years after that, the president came out in favor of it. Throughout the 1920s, lynching decreased drastically as local and state governments took the crisis more seriously. After decades of writing, researching, talking, traveling, working on her argument, finding relevant data, testing different avenues, pressuring various friendly and unfriendly actors, and waging campaigns on multiple fronts, Wells won.

We remember Martin Luther King Jr. for his cinematic dragon-slaying—his iconic speeches and confrontations—but what's lost is all the long-haul work that queued up those moments. King makes clear in *Stride Toward Freedom*, his memoir of the Montgomery bus boycott, just how much time he spent in the mundane work of winning the community's trust, joining local organizations, weaving together coalitions through multiple meetings, and planning efficient public gatherings.

We often forget that King first came to Montgomery because he committed to being the pastor at a local Baptist church. The whole beginning of his memoir is about the not-so-thrilling work of forming church committees: a religious education committee, a social service committee, a scholarship fundraising committee, and a cultural committee. Early on in Montgomery, he wrote, most of his time was spent performing marriages and funerals, preparing the weekly service, visiting the sick, and attending various church planning meetings. "Almost every week I attended from five to ten such group meetings," he wrote, "and most of my early evenings were consumed in this fashion."

Why was King trusted to lead the boycott? Because he had spent the months leading up to it religiously attending various local organizations' meetings. He first joined the NAACP's local branch and helped them with fundraising. He then joined the Alabama Council on Human Relations, an interracial group of reverends helping to fight for racial equality in Alabama. He then started going to meetings for the Citizens Coordinating Committee, a group formed to build unity among local leaders. The story we're told—about how "Rosa Parks sat down and the community stood up"—leaves out the most important part: Parks, King, and hundreds of other committed people had put in the week-in, week-out work of sustaining local organizations before the boycott ever started. Parks's heroic confrontation was the spark—but sparks go nowhere without the long-haul gathering of tinder.

And that doesn't even include all the meetings that went into building the organizations that made up the coordinating bodies that hosted the meetings that sustained the boycott. The only reason King's congregation at Dexter Avenue Baptist Church was ready to be politicized is because the church's prior pastor, Vernon Johns, had been organizing and activating them for years. The only reason there was a Women's Political Council for King to coordinate with was because nine years prior, forty-one women came together to found it. The local branch of the International Union of Bricklayers gave King office space—and the only reason they were able to do that was because local bricklayers built and sustained a union hall over the previous four decades. Though she's remembered as a dragon-slayer, Rosa Parks herself was also a long-haul hero: When she was arrested, she was already a decade into being the elected secretary of the Montgomery branch of the NAACP.

The bus boycott ended up lasting 381 days. You can sustain a week of action based on a passionate reaction to a dramatic incident.

But to sustain a thirteen-month-long campaign, you need something deeper than reaction—you need commitment. It reminds me of something the civil rights organizer Ella Baker once wrote in a report back to her team headquarters in the 1940s: "I must leave now for one of those small church night meetings which are usually more exhausting than the immediate returns seem to warrant, but it's a part of the spade work, so let it be." Spadework—preparing the soil for action—is what long-haul heroism is all about.

In the 1950s and '60s, one person might've been dispatched to a new city to help activate it for civil rights. They wouldn't know anyone except the one family who would sponsor them, Movement veteran Doris Crenshaw remembers. That's when the spadework began: growing a speck of a campaign, one meeting at a time. A person would find energy in any progress they'd make. "If you have two of you and you get two more people to be engaged," she said, that was a start. "Jesus only had twelve disciples. You just have to keep on going . . . It's not a sprint, it's a long-distance run."

I once visited the home of Medgar Evers, one of the legendary martyrs of the civil rights movement. The sign in front of his house reads: "Medgar and Myrlie Evers moved into this home with their children—Darrell and Reena—in 1955 after Medgar became Mississippi's first NAACP Field Secretary. . . . Just after midnight, on June 12, 1963, he was assassinated in the driveway as he returned from a meeting."

We are told that what made Evers brave—what made him a hero—is that he was killed for his cause. But we can't overlook that last part of the sign: that Evers was killed "as he returned from a meeting." It is noble to give your life to a cause—but it is even nobler to give your daily life to it.

6

A Tour of the Counterculture

I once saw a sign in a bar that read: "GUILT: Invented by Jews. Perfected by Catholics." It could be my family's crest. I descend from a line of Catholics and Jews who took seriously the idea of being *implicated*. Today, *implicated* is a simple synonym for *guilty*, but it has an older definition: to be "folded in" or "entwined." Sometimes, in my family, this sense of implication has taken the form of our modern sense of guilt: abiding worry about whether we are wronging others. But most of the time, it has meant something less neurotic: feeling a sense of obligation to the people around us and around the world. In its most elevated form, it is a sense of feeling what the great rabbi Abraham Joshua Heschel meant when he said that "indifference to evil is worse than evil itself; that in a free society, some are guilty, but all are responsible."

My grandmother, Clara Lewe Gubbins, was the longest-residing citizen of her Illinois community. She spent eight decades—from the 1920s to the 2000s—in the town of Riverside, with college and World War II her only absences. She raised seven children and spent her life serving her local Catholic parish, local civic groups, and local Democratic Party. As a decades-long member of the local Legion of Mary, she made hundreds of house visits to neighbors in need. Inspired by Eleanor Roosevelt, she wrote hundreds of letters to elected officials, sharing her praise, criticism, and advice.

Her father, John C. Lewe, was a judge and a civic leader in town. My family found a letter Judge Lewe wrote to his daughter-in-law in the late 1950s where he expressed concern about how people were becoming too "engrossed in their petty affairs" and therefore indifferent to public affairs. "The government is not 'they,'" he wrote. "It is 'us.' All of us must play our part." After a few paragraphs spent decrying how McCarthyism was ruining "everything that Franklin Roosevelt stood for," he ends the letter saying: "Do not get angry with your neighbors [if] they do not share your views. Try to reason with them, but in any event be patient and tolerant and neighborly. Eventually you will win their respect."

My mom inherited these qualities—a sense of place, dedication to political values, and unwavering neighborliness. She spent her career advocating for children and students, all while maintaining what my sister and I sometimes refer to as "the factory": a home whirring at all hours with gift projects at various stages of development. Knitted hats for babies, art kits for the school down the road, brownies for coworkers having a hard time, clippings of news articles she thinks we might find interesting, and stacks of poems she knows our friends will like—no moment is too small to be acknowledged. She possesses the increasingly rare quality of being both an outspoken politico and an empathetic listener. Even the neighbors who do not share her well-trumpeted views can't resist her open heart and sympathetic ear.

My dad, the son of Jewish immigrants, grew up on the East End of Pittsburgh. The joy of his childhood was Emma Kaufmann Camp, a summer camp created by local department store magnates to help poor Jewish city kids get fresh air. My dad spent over a decade returning to the camp—first as a camper, then as a "kitchen boy," then as a counselor, and finally as its nature director. The directors of the camp were social workers, so he wanted to study social work, too. When he arrived at Antioch College in 1960, he initially studied sociology—the closest major to "social work."

To attend Antioch in the early sixties was a uniquely civic experience. The student body prided itself in, in the words of the school's president, "being willing to risk the challenge to convention in order that they may have the opportunity to lead in humane causes and in the solution of human problems." The school's motto, originating from its founder Horace Mann, left no doubt about what was expected of Antioch graduates: "Be ashamed to die until you have won some victory for humanity." To top it all off, Martin Luther King Jr. was my dad's graduation speaker. (His wife, Coretta Scott, was an Antioch alum.) He called on graduates of the Antioch class of 1965 to "develop a world perspective" and a "divine discontent" to injustice.

I once found a letter my dad wrote right after graduating where he said that his goal in life was "to be able, in a small minute way, to act on the human crisis of the 20th century." In the spirit of King's call to develop "a world perspective," he became an activist anthropologist, spending half a century founding nonprofits, hosting conferences, writing books and reports, connecting groups, and fighting zealous battles inside powerful institutions for the sake of helping increase the voice that indigenous communities had in the forces that governed their lives. When he died ten years ago and the letters from his friends poured in, I had to look up what *indefatigable* meant, because so many people called him that. But when I was growing up, all I knew of this work was the monk-like routines I witnessed for twenty years: him waking up at the same time each morning and eating the same whole-grain cereal; him paging through some report, pen in hand, underlining important sections and scrawling notes in the margins; him packing and unpacking his clothes in the exact same way for trips around the world. Before I understood the content of my dad's work, I understood the steadiness of it.

I also grew up in a town—Falls Church, Virginia—that had a strong identity. It had a small school system and a rich civic life, especially for children: Boy and Girl Scouts, Operation EarthWatch, youth soccer and Little League every Saturday morning, the *Falls Church News-Press* at everyone's door every Thursday, the fall festival in October, the Memorial Day parade in May. Behind every beloved institution in town was a dedicated person. Howard Herman helmed the weekly farmers market. Nikki and Ed Henderson were in charge of the annual blues festival. Nick Benton kept the *News-Press* running. Barb Cram kept the local art shows going. Sue John kept the preschool open.

Annette Mills and Dave Eckert were our community's super-citizens. Annette somehow turned our town's tiny recycling and litter-prevention program into a fun community endeavor—complete with school clubs, picnics, and T-shirts—in which hundreds of us kids participated. Dave was a one-man civic incubator who helped launch one local institution after another, from an Urban Stream

Task Force to a New Year's Eve block party in the center of town to a street festival celebrating the Black history of Falls Church. Annette and Dave were masters at drawing people deeper into the community: Annette would mix in local history stories with her litter cleanup walks; Dave would make documentaries about streams in town to try to get us all to pay better attention to Falls Church's natural world.

Dave's commitment to our town actually started with a much smaller commitment, to a tiny tract of land in the middle of town. Thirty years ago, Dave had gotten word that a little wooded area with a small stream running through it was at risk of being sold off to a private developer. He went straight to the press and kicked up a fuss with the Falls Church Tree Commission. The land should be made into a public park, he argued. "I had never engaged in this type of community advocacy and overplayed my cards quite a bit," he admits. Town leaders, in Dave's words, "set him straight," issuing him a challenge: "If you really want something done, you need to join us and help rather than tell us to do something."

He took them up on it and joined the local Village Preservation and Improvement Society (VPIS). But soon Dave's tiny crusade to save a little tract of land spiraled. Through VPIS, Dave started working on other community betterment projects, from a booth at the farmers market to a house concert series. "I was in way over my head," he remembers, "and thoroughly enjoying it."

Annette says that the secret to her and her husband's civic perseverance is "the social component." If your civic work is not building relationships, she insists, it's not going to work. Annette's projects snowball—and Annette stays inspired—because she designs them so that neighbors get to know each other through their work. It's why, for example, instead of simply asking the city government to plant more trees, she started a Neighborhood Tree Program in town to help neighbors plant trees together—and, in the process, bond as a neighborhood. When you're bringing people together and having fun doing it, Dave chimes in, the commitments help you "feed yourself." Community work gives their life meaning: "I want to go to my grave saying I did everything I possibly could to move this society, this world, in a better direction for all," Annette said.

In the early 2000s, Annette and Dave moved away, but many of their local projects live on in Falls Church. As I was writing this book, I would take breaks and find inspiration by walking around a wonderful public park near my house. It's a little tract of woods with a small stream running through it, preserved for the public's enjoyment—one of the many fruits of Dave and Annette's dedication.

As I grew older, I was drawn to similarly committed people. In college, I sought out long-haul heroes as mentors, from a bellicose activist who has spent half a century fighting abuses of corporate power to a quirky social scientist who has investigated American social trends for decades to a stubborn philosopher who toiled in obscurity for years in an attempt to illuminate a new way of understanding society.

The more the culture seemed to devalue faithfulness, the more the dedicated stood out to me: the strange man who played Americana covers every Monday night for years for the regulars at the bar down the street, the neighbor who got everyone she knew involved with the local shelter, the classmate who visited their elderly friend religiously, the coworker who kept her family traditions going. I started observing how the things that enlivened me the most—the old pals and the old haunts, the seasonal rituals and the never-ending inside jokes, the cozy books and the overplayed songs on the piano—all stemmed from commitment.

I also started noticing that every time someone was talking about some person they respected, it was usually because they admired the person's commitment to something or other. The neighbor who went all-in on the banjo or screenwriting or carpentry, the couple who set down roots somewhere and started building a family, the friend who so doubled-down on starting a farm or becoming a pastor or learning Brazilian jiujitsu that they made everyone think "wow, she's really going for it"—those were the people earning deep admiration. It showed up even with people nobody really liked but everybody grudgingly respected. "Can't stand her, but you can't deny she's a real artist"; "He's hard to talk to, but you gotta respect the man's commitment to the campaign"; "I don't like his views, but he's a devoted father." It's the commitment that shines through.

As I piled up a collection of these examples—while at the same time noticing how much our culture pulled in the opposite direction—I began seeing this group of solid people in our liquid world as something resembling a counterculture. In resisting the pull to infinitely browse, they blaze an alternative path of life.

There are many routes into this rebellion, because there are many particular things to which one can commit. You do not have to be a crusader like Ida B. Wells or Medgar Evers, or a civic superstar like Annette Mills or Dave Eckert, to join up. Causes are but one thing to which you can dedicate yourself. There are also crafts and projects, places and communities, institutions and people that need our dedication. If you're wondering where you might fit into this Counterculture of Commitment, you'll be happy to know that there are, ironically, plenty of options.

Citizens

In 1983, while Evan Wolfson was a student in law school, he wrote his third-year paper on the constitutional right to same-sex marriage. It is hard to overstate how much of a fringe position this idea was at the time—it hadn't even won the support of the broader queer community yet. Most gay rights lawyers in the early 1980s were just fighting for basic legal protections, like freedom from being evicted or fired for being gay.

But Wolfson got to work. After a *thirty-two-year* battle—after a decade of helping convince gay rights groups to launch a marriage campaign, then a decade of getting just one state to fully recognize gay marriage, and then another decade of building state-by-state campaigns to popularize gay marriage across the country—Wolfson witnessed the Supreme Court legalize gay marriage for every American. The path of pushing his idea from the least consequential form of legal writing (a law school paper) to the most consequential (a Supreme Court decision) was winding. One moment, he was winning a long-shot case to recognize gay marriage in Hawaii; the next, he was fighting off a national backlash. One day he'd be turned down by fellow activists when recruiting support for a marriage strategy; the next, he was founding Freedom to Marry, a well-funded campaign to fight the marriage battle in the states.

When somebody pushed his buttons, or when others were being "too timid or too difficult," Evan read history. Lincoln, Gandhi, King, the women's suffrage movement, the emancipation fight, even ancient history—reading about past struggles gave him great consolation.

"You have to believe you can win," he said. "You have to believe things can change, and you have to pace yourself and be patient yet tenacious."

In the decades of ups and downs, Wolfson had rarely cried. He was known for being succinct, stoic, and lawyerly. But in June 2015, as he walked to his desk to read the *Obergefell* decision, "the tears were coming." A flood of memories came to him as he read: "Every paragraph reminded me of an argument I had with someone, or somebody I worked with who had died, or what I was doing during this particular piece of the fight—*this year, this state, this struggle*."

In 2016, having succeeded after three decades of sustained commitment, Wolfson dissolved his organization. "A campaign is driving a strategy to a goal," Evan insists. When the goal is achieved, the campaign is over. It's a good reminder that change-making need not always be about a never-ending, tragic relationship to an unchanging order; it can be about a discrete strategy aimed at a culminating outcome. Just because challenges take time to tackle—sometimes even thirty-two years—doesn't mean they're not finite.

Evan's form of long-haul heroism is the most recognizable: commitment to causes. This is the work of *citizens*—people who take ownership over the fate of society and work to push society in a direction they believe will benefit it. Citizens mix vision with first steps—lofty ideals about what is just with concrete actions that move communities and institutions in the direction of those ideals. Commitments to causes sound nice after you win, but along the way, it's difficult. We call people who have won their causes "heroes," but we call people who are in the middle of their causes "crazy."

Lori Wallach, the founder of Public Citizen's Global Trade Watch, has been called every name in the book for her advocacy. In the early 1990s, Lori was working on food safety issues in DC. She had learned the rhythm of congressional hearings: Some regulation would be proposed to protect food safety. A moderate group would testify to say that the legislation was good. An industry group would testify to say it would be disastrous and "the end of all commerce." And then Lori would say that the bill didn't go far enough. But one day, while a pesticide bill was being discussed, something changed.

The moderate group said, "This bill's about right."

Lori got up and said, "This bill isn't good enough."

And then the pesticide lobbyist got up and *didn't* say, "This is the end of the world." Rather, he said, "You can't pass this bill. It's illegal under the rules of the Codex Alimentarius. If you want this, it has to be written into the multilateral trade agreement."

What the heck is that man talking about? Lori recalls thinking. *He must have had a six-martini lunch.* But she looked up the Codex Alimentarius and discovered that it was a part of an international trade agreement on pesticide standards. The corporate lobbyist was right: Congress couldn't change the bill without renegotiating the international agreement.

A few months later, the same thing happened at a meat hearing. The guy from the National Cattlemen's Beef Association said Congress couldn't require "country of origin" labeling on meat under the North American Free Trade Agreement.

"It was like the second ping on that raw nerve that had been exposed in the previous hearing," Lori recalls. Something fishy was going on.

"I was posted as the guard of food safety at the front door, yet while I'm standing there watching any suspicious character walk by, there is a back door," she explains. "I don't know what the back door is, but it's related to trade."

That moment, a quarter century ago, was the beginning of Lori's long haul to understand and watchdog international trade agreements for corporate malfeasance. Someone needed to "translate all the technical craziness," she said, "and that was me." At the beginning, Lori had little knowledge of foreign policy at the time—and few on the public-interest side of trade battles knew what was going on. But she had the analytical skills from law school to dive into complex texts and start unpacking them. This wasn't easy—the global trade agreements, Lori explains, were "intentionally inaccessible legal texts." The other side could buy dozens of people to understand them. All she had was herself, at least at first.

But she dove in anyway. She would take whole chapters of giant trade agreements—with titles like "Sanitary Standards"—and meticulously translate what they meant for, say, food safety, pesticides, meat inspection, or labeling. The goal was to explain to people how it would affect "what was happening on your kitchen table, right in your house, right with your kid." Over the following decades, she repeated this process with trade deal after trade deal.

During the nineties, most of the establishment was against Lori. She lists off the critiques: "We were wrong; we were isolationists; we were protectionists." She ruffled so many feathers that when she was put on the cover of a major foreign policy magazine, two people resigned from the magazine's board. At one point, after losing two significant congressional votes, she started crying at work. She felt like she was done—and met up with her mentor Ralph Nader to get some advice. He told her she needed to think longer term.

"You basically are being pursued by a steamroller of corporate power in a narrow alley," he told her. "And you can either lie down and let it roll over you or you can keep figuring out how you're going to jam it, get it sideways, or throw sand in the gears. And once you actually stop it, you'll be in the position to start turning it around and winning the policies you want."

Lori and her small international network—from Malaysian consumer unions to Indian food justice activists to Uruguayan journalists—stayed relentless. By doggedly gathering evidence and refusing to take powerful interests at their word, they got a foothold in the conversation. By the end of the nineties, they had gone from being called cranks to being seen as reasonable critics in a mainstream debate. By the mid-2010s, over twenty years after Lori began her fight, she and her allies were finally able to stop a corporate-driven trade deal. At the time I talked to Lori, twenty-seven years after she began her journey, she felt like she had finally reached the moment of halting the steamroller. Now she could start on her next three-decade walk: turning it around.

Patriots

Another form of long-haul heroism is commitment to places and the communities that populate them. People who make these commitments are *patriots*. Patriotism is a fraught idea today, polarized by misuse. Politicians have used it to pass their latest bill or cover up their latest scandal. Flag-waving nationalists have used it to browbeat dissidents into submission. And now many see it as a shallow virtue—the stuff of halftime shows and parade bunting, not serious dedication.

But we shouldn't be so quick to abandon the idea of love of place. My favorite 4th of July song is "I Am a Patriot," originally written by E Street Band member Steven Van Zandt. The chorus nails what patriotism can mean: "I am a patriot and I love my country because my country is all I know...I've got nowhere else to go." In this reading of patriotism, you do not love your country because it's "the best." You don't love your country because it's uniquely great or just, or because you believe your fellow countrymen deserve any more care than any other people do. Rather, you love it because it's the one you are part of—the one you know, the one you're bound up in. It's not the patriotism of domination and exclusion, but the patriotism of dedication to a place and its people.

This type of patriotism is easier to find on a smaller scale. The ardent localist Bill Kauffman writes about the "profoundly un-imperial patriotism" of America's small towns and neighborhoods—not "the sham patriotism of the couch-sitter who sings 'God Bless America' as the bombs light up his television" but the love of "music, poetry, places, quirks and commonalities, historical crotchets, holy fools, and eminent Kansans." It's the patriotism that preserves *heterogeneity*— the flourishing of various beloved places, whose quirky ways of doing things are not ironed out for the sake of the whole, but treated as (in the words of Simone Weil) "treasures of infinite value and rarity, worth tending like the most delicate plants."

But patriotism—even local patriotism—need not be a static exercise. As the philosopher Richard Rorty has argued, a certain level of patriotism is an ingredient for making change. "National pride is to countries what self-respect is to individuals," he wrote: a "necessary condition for self-improvement." Too much pride makes you arrogant. But too little makes it difficult to "display moral courage" or summon the resources and energy to transform things. This is why, he argues, the great works of American reform—from Lincoln's and King's speeches to *The Grapes of Wrath* and *The Jungle*—launched their critiques with a tone of real concern for a beloved country, not cynical disdain for a lost cause. It's hard to change a place without being part of it.

Perhaps the greatest living American thinker on this deeper sense of patriotism is Wendell Berry. Berry's a farmer, philosopher, activist, novelist, essayist, and poet. He's won the National Humanities Medal and been lauded for his writing on culture and the environment. But what's most important to know about Berry is that he's done it all from—and for—one place: his hometown of Port Royal, Kentucky.

Borrowing terms from his mentor Wallace Stegner, Berry writes that there are two types of people in the world: "boomers" and "stickers." Boomers are mobile, moving from place to place to seize opportunity. At their worst, they "pillage and run," motivated by money, property, and power. The stickers are "those who settle, and love the life they have made and the place they have made it in." They put down roots and are motivated by affection—"by such love for a place and its life that they want to preserve it and remain in it."

Berry laments that our modern culture promotes booming over sticking. Young people from rural families, he admits, have always gone "off to the cities, not to return." But now it feels "that this is what they should do"—that the norm is to leave and not return. The goal—everywhere, not just in rural communities—has become not just to succeed your parents but to also supersede them. We are educated, he decries, to trade our home communities for earning money "in a provisional future that has nothing to do with place or community."

In his writing, Berry shares with boomers what the stickers know:

that committing to a place is not confining, but freeing. The life of a boomer, the critic George Scialabba writes of Berry's philosophy, is defined by abstract, institutional authorities—"university, corporation, profession, government." When you are stuck in such a "nebulous grid" of "shadowy bureaucracy," it's hard to find your bearings, measure your progress, or foster affection in your daily life. Stickers, on the other hand, get to deal with a stable set of the real, particular things—the people, the buildings, the nature, the culture—that make up the place to which they have committed. It's not constant worry about "How am I doing?" or "Am I on the inside or the outside?" but rather the slow and steady progress of deepening relationships with your particular neighbors, increasing familiarity with your particular surroundings, and mastering the crafts of your particular calling.

And it's not just that commitment to place allows you to see every splendid detail of your corner of the world. It's also that commitment gives you the time to see the *wholeness*—the interconnectivity of your place. The boomers are constantly dissecting and analyzing the different elements of the world—they need to in order to manage the enormous social systems they helm. The stickers, on the other hand, can see how everything in their particular place fits together—how the land and the climate, the plants and the animals and the people, the buildings and the businesses and the traditions, all interact with one another. When you can see this wholeness, you can solve local problems in a deep way. This kind of problem-solving isn't accomplished through one-off data-driven "cures," but through the healing work of making a damaged ecosystem whole again.

Berry has a beautiful image that ties his localist philosophy together. At his grandfather's farm, he recalls, there was an old bucket hanging on a fence post. It hadn't been moved in years. Over time, spring rain, autumn leaves, and winter snow had fallen inside many times over. Nuts had been carried into it by squirrels, and some mice had eaten some of the nuts and left the shells. Some of the leaves had rotted, and insects flew in and died. Birds scratched into it and left behind a feather or two. Eventually, the bottom of the bucket was filled with several inches of rich soil.

"What is going on in that bucket is the most momentous thing I know, the greatest miracle that I have ever heard of," Berry wrote. "It is making earth."

Stable communities, to Berry, are like the bucket. They collect stories as they fall through time. They preserve "memories, ways, and skills." They accumulate lore and song. They make sure that local knowledge is "remembered or recorded, handed down, pondered, corrected, practiced, and refined over a long time." And, eventually, what comes out of the compost is a rich local culture fertile for planting and harvest. But it doesn't happen automatically.

"A human community," Berry wrote, "must exert a sort of centripetal force, holding local soil and local memory in place." Too often today, places do not have enough people committed to them—enough patriots dedicated to being vessels of local culture-making—and, as a result, many local cultures and communities are dissipating.

Some dismiss Berry's ideas as being relevant only to a small set of nostalgic farmers, but I think his message applies to all kinds of communities. On the surface, Pierce Freelon—the newest member of the Durham, North Carolina, city council—could not be any more different from Berry. He lives in a good-size city, not a small town. He's the son of a Black architect and a jazz vocalist, not white farmers. And his primary form of expression is music and filmmaking, not essays and novels. But he's just as much of a local patriot as Berry is.

Freelon has lived in Durham for his whole life. When he was young, he remembers wanting to hit the road and "see what else was out there." And he did for a bit—but the more he traveled, the more he came to appreciate how special his hometown was. He started seeing the folks he grew up with become business owners and community leaders. He started discovering more about the heroes of Durham's history: Ernie Barnes, the pro football player turned groundbreaking painter; Pauli Murray, the crusading feminist and civil rights lawyer whose work influenced the *Brown vs. Board of Education* decision; André Leon Talley, the grandson of a sharecropper who became editor of *Vogue*. He started falling in love again with this strange city—his creative, Southern, progressive, Bible Belt hometown.

Pierce is a talented artist, so I asked him whether he ever felt limited by not living in a city where young people go to "make it"—the LAs and Brooklyns of the world. He actually wrote a song about the feeling, appropriately titled "Brooklyn." In it, he's in a relationship with a North Carolinian, but while visiting New York he meets an interesting, attractive, mysterious Brooklynite who tempts him away. But by the end of the song, he can't stop pining for the "fireflies in a jar, poked holes in the top," the "blue skies and the hurricanes," and the "corn bread, catfish, and collard greens" of his hometown. He tried to escape to Brooklyn, but Carolina was on his mind and heart—so he packed his bags and headed home.

Pierce said he likes to remind his fellow artists that just because some other place has more resources doesn't mean it has more resources for *you*. "A fifteen-minute subway ride from an industry that has a gatekeeper that might not let you in anyway" might pale in comparison to a place where you can get to know everybody. A person with roots in a relatively under-resourced place can go toe-to-toe with somebody who doesn't have any roots in a highly resourced place. That's why Pierce feels comfortable living by his grandma's maxim: "Bloom where you're planted." Whenever he gets antsy about whether bigger, better things are out there for him, Pierce reminds himself that those feelings of anxiety—that he's not good enough, that he's not doing things right, that he's not seizing all opportunities—have nothing to do with where he lives. "Those things are not going to go anywhere just because you moved to a different place," he insists. "The key to achieving peace and success is to define what success means for yourself." Enough is as good as feast, he tells himself. We get "just as full from a hearty meal, locally sourced, than we do at a lavish fancy restaurant."

Some patriots are committed not to a specific place but rather to a community. When Peggy Berryhill was five years old, living in low-income housing in Oakland, she remembers watching *Davy Crockett* with her dad. In one episode of the show, the famed frontiersman—who had inspired thousands of children Peggy's age to wear coonskin hats—gets in a battle with the Muscogee, the nation to which Peggy and her family belong. She remembers how ridiculous the Muscogee were portrayed—they were "dressed like plains people in fringed buckskin and big stupid war paint on their face, with long braids." Worse, in the episode, Crockett single-handedly defeated three or four Muscogee men in battle. It was at that point, at a young age, that Peggy made a decision: "If there's anything I can do in my life, I'm going to change the stereotype of Indians."

And that's what Peggy, for the past half century, has worked to do. Earning the moniker "the First Lady of Native Radio," she has spent decades collecting, producing, and broadcasting hundreds of hours of interviews with Native people.

In the early 1970s, a radio show dedicated to Native issues was lying fallow on KPFA, the community radio station in Berkeley, California. Peggy, a student journalist at the time, took it over. Serving audiences from Fresno to Reno, she went around, mic in hand, to all the local Native community events she could get to. Her show, *Living on Indian Time*, soon became a hit with both Native and non-Native listeners around the region. Over the coming decades, Peggy's show became one of the de facto community centers for the wave of Native empowerment campaigns in the late twentieth century. She interviewed activists like Cherokee leader Wilma Mankiller and Pawnee attorney John Echohawk to teach listeners about the various active struggles for Native civil rights and self-determination. But she also interviewed nonactivists, too—she wanted to show the diversity of Native luminaries, from the Oneida comedian Charlie Hill, to the Cree singer-songwriter Buffy Sainte-Marie, to the Sioux actor Floyd Westerman.

Peggy once asked a tribal leader where he saw Native folks in five years. (When she was young, she recalls with a grin, that seemed like a long time.) He responded that he saw "Indians owning their own banks and Indian airlines, and Indians basically doing everything that anybody else could do—but it was going to be Indianized, with indigenous principles." She remembers being so taken by how future-oriented the sentiment was. She wanted to capture that spirit in her show: that Native culture was not frozen in amber, but was a living thing with a future. That's what real patriots do—they are not committed to some frozen idea of what a community is; they are committed to real people in an evolving community. Almost fifty years after grabbing her first microphone in 1973, Peggy is still going, hosting interviews every weekday morning on Northern

California's KGUA, breaking stereotypes, raising up her community, and—like Berry's bucket—helping sustain that centripetal force that keeps a people together.

Builders

Some people's dedication takes the form of turning dreams into realities. This is the work of *builders*. Like the citizen, they have a vision of the future—and aim to do the long-haul work of making that vision real. But instead of pulling or pushing some existing part of the world toward their vision, they prefigure their vision in miniature by creating something.

Ten years ago, Irene Li and her siblings moved back home to be closer to their parents. To keep themselves occupied, they came up with a plan to start a food truck. They wanted to continue the legacy of their Chinese immigrant grandparents, who made it in America by starting a restaurant. In 2012, they opened the Mei Mei Street Kitchen food truck in downtown Boston. Irene worked to make sure their operation lived up to her commitment to food justice. She wanted the produce to be sourced locally, the animals used for the meat raised on pastures, and the average downtown worker in Boston to be able to afford eating their food a couple of times a week. The truck was such a hit that Irene and her family opened a brick-and-mortar restaurant a year later.

When they opened Mei Mei on Park Drive in Boston, they wanted the restaurant to embody their family tradition of hospitality. The word really means something to Irene: it's "this idea that we are responsible to one another." Hospitality's the virtue of "anticipating what people need and giving freely of what you have." If I were to

93

visit her mom's house, Irene told me, she "would ask you if you've eaten and she's going to refill your glass a bunch of times and she's going to notice that you're wearing a T-shirt and you have goose bumps and she's going to find you a sweater." She adds: "She's not even really going to ask—it's just going to happen." That was the spirit she wanted at Mei Mei.

Sometimes Irene feels bad about being tied down—it's hard, for example, to take long vacations when the restaurant always needs helming. But at the end of the day, it's hard for her "to imagine being satisfied with life without being deeply committed to some form of work." The restaurant has become part of her public identity. Having been in the business for almost a decade, she now sits on the boards of various local nonprofits, including one that incubates emerging food businesses. It's still weird for her to hear people say at meetings, "Oh, you know, Mei Mei has been doing this for years, you should ask them," because her reputation as an industry veteran, she tells me, has "sort of snuck up on" her.

What's strange about building a restaurant is that it requires putting on a great show one day, and then the next day starting all over again from scratch. In processing the repetitiveness of her commitment, Irene has been taken by the idea of "track record." Consistent employee satisfaction, consistent customer reviews, consistent community leadership—that's how she measures progress now.

"When we are able to establish that we do something a certain way and we've done it that way for a long time," she said, "that holds real value."

Stewards

If everyone were a builder and reformer, the world wouldn't work. We need some people, at least some of the time, to be *stewards*—to keep what already exists going. As Andrew Russell and Lee Vinsel argue in their viral *Aeon* essay, "Hail the Maintainers," our culture overvalues innovation—the crusaders and creators—while undervaluing the maintenance that comes after "the big, new idea" has been realized. Innovation, they observe, is only the first phase of technological development. Technologies have a lifecycle—and most of that lifecycle is the work of maintenance. Cleaning; replacing parts; updating software; fixing glitches; even sustaining the human programs that organize and train folks to clean, replace parts, update software, and fix glitches—all of that work is done by maintainers, not innovators. Around most new technologies is a maintenance network that makes it function: Every iPhone needs a well-maintained communication network to work, every fancy showerhead needs a well-maintained water network to work, and every Tesla needs a well-maintained highway network to work. And most of what makes modern life modern—subways, bridges, pipes, HVAC systems—are not that new. We don't notice them, Russell and Vinsel point out, because it's the maintainers—the landscapers, the mechanics, the IT support teams, the hospital technicians—who keep them whirring, not innovators.

And it isn't just technological maintenance that keeps society functioning—it's all the maintenance that goes into social systems, too. We need people to maintain relationships, tend to rituals, enforce norms, and train new members. I think often about all the maintenance that goes into keeping "the law" running—all the lawyers and judges, bailiffs and court reporters, legal libraries and law schools, paperwork and buildings. Even the smallest social systems—the neighborhood book club or prayer group—need people to show up. I once saw a friend grapple with whether she should go to the monthly book talk that she helped start at her local library. It was raining and cold and she wasn't in the mood. And then after a long pause, she said, "I guess I ought to," and she grabbed her coat and went to the library.

"I guess I ought to" keeps civilization from falling apart.

The spirit of stewardship, the localist writer Mark T. Mitchell wrote, is "an indispensable feature of a thriving culture." All those "institutions, ways of thinking, stories, songs, traditions, practices" that we inherit—they need tending to. If there are not enough people committed to stewarding them, we lose them. But stewardship doesn't mean preserving something behind glass—it means keeping something alive, like you would a plant or an animal. Stewardship is active, Mitchell explains—it involves reflecting on your inheritance's "strengths and weaknesses, trying to improve it as we are attending to it, and then carefully passing it on to the next generation." Reception in gratitude, loving stewardship, and enthusiastic transmission—that's how a culture survives.

Gabriela Grajeda moved to my part of Virginia in 2003. She wanted to stay close to her Bolivian heritage, so she joined up with a Bolivian dance troupe in our area, Alma Boliviana. It was isolating for her to come here—there was a much smaller Hispanic population than in Los Angeles, where she had lived before. Her dance troupe was a familiar community, filled with people who had similar backgrounds and similar passions. It felt like home.

What Gabriela loves about Alma Boliviana is what Mark T.

Mitchell was talking about: It's a group that inherits, stewards, and passes down her culture. Many people in Alma haven't lived in Bolivia—only their parents have. So the group keeps the spirit of the culture alive thousands of miles away from where it originated. The dances are difficult. But when Gabriela learns and performs them, she is enacting her culture. The difficulty is part of the pride.

The dances are also an excuse to talk about Bolivia. "People ask why we do each dance and the origin behind each dance," she says, and that gives her an opportunity to share her heritage. "Each dance is a story unto itself," she explains, and there's a "really fascinating history behind each and behind the costumes, too." Through the songs, the dancers learn a bit of Quechua, an indigenous language, as well as some Bolivian slang.

Stewardship isn't easy, Gabriela said. There's always the need to iron out group tensions, come up with clever ways to raise money, and recruit new members. But after a few seasons of doing that, Gabriela has built up resilience. She sees it as her duty to keep the group going. "We're the oldest group in the area, and for that reason I wouldn't like to see it die," she said. "It's a sense of purpose, a sense of responsibility to continue something."

The textbook stewardship profession may be clergy, who carry an entire religious tradition, keep it alive, and transmit it to their congregation every week. Rabbi Amy Schwartzman has been with my town's synagogue for thirty years. Part of her work is carrying forth traditions and rituals—bar and bat mitzvahs, weddings, funerals, and of course annual holidays and weekly Shabbat services. Another part is talking to people about their relationship with their faith—and often, their doubts. Rabbi Schwartzman says her goal is frequently to keep wavering congregants sufficiently "tethered to

Judaism" so that when they come to a point in their life where they are ready to explore their faith more, "they'll know that Judaism will be there for them."

Perhaps the most important part of her work is training children in the faith—and with nine hundred students, Rabbi Schwartzman runs the second-largest Jewish religious school in the country. When kids are preparing for their bar and bat mitzvahs, they are not just learning Hebrew, she told me—"they're processing for a year what it means to *become* a bar or bat mitzvah" (a "child of the command-ment"). Often this work involves challenging young people to take on their own commitments—to ask themselves "When are you pre-pared to put your tradition above yourself?" And the educational work doesn't stop with kids. Rabbi Schwartzman is always working to call all members of her congregation to "aspirational Judaism"— to be asking, "What ways do the choices you make influence the future of Judaism and your future as a Jew?"

Rabbi Schwartzman joined the rabbinate because she loves this work of ritual, guidance, and religious education. For her, that part of stewardship isn't a burden—it's a joy. But being the head of a congre-gation comes not just with the heartfelt work of spiritual stewardship but also the often boring work of logistical stewardship—holding planning meetings, going over financial documents, fundraising, ap-plying for building permits, and more. But she likes to remind her-self that her commitment to her congregation—and to preserving Judaism generally—means that this tedious, logistical work is just as much part of being a rabbi as teaching the kids Judaism.

All that work by all the rabbis like Rabbi Schwartzman in all the synagogues around the world keeps a millennia-old tradition alive. "One of the things I always say at the Passover seder," Rabbi

Schwartzman tells me, "is to think about the image of the Jews all over the world who are doing exactly what you're doing. And to think about how your grandparents, your great-grandparents said these very words. And hopefully so will your children and your grandchildren and people who you will never know." After a sigh, she adds: "That is a big feeling."

Artisans

To hone a craft is long-haul work, too. The amateur baker honing his bread, the classical guitarist honing her fingerpicking, the teacher honing their teaching style—it all takes time and repetition. These days, you hear about the commitment to craft as putting in your "ten thousand hours." I like New York horticulturalist Andi Pettis's maxim better: One of her gardening mentors explained to her that "you're not a real gardener until you've killed at least one hundred plants." This long-haul craft-honing is the work of *artisans*.

Mickey Raphael has been touring for decades as Willie Nelson's harmonica guy. Mickey didn't set out to be a world-renowned harmonica player. He played guitar like everybody else growing up in the 1960s. But one day in high school, at a coffeehouse in Dallas, he heard Donnie Brooks playing blues harmonica. He was so taken by Brooks's playing that he thought at that moment, with complete certainty: "Okay, this is what I want to do." So he found a Hohner Marine Band harmonica, started playing blues licks, and that was that.

Mickey had inherited a dedication to craftsmanship from his father, who was a custom furniture builder. But Mickey flunked woodshop, so he wasn't going to take up the family trade. His father would have to settle for Mickey dedicating his gene for obsession to the harmonica, which he was soon carrying everywhere he went. He was a loner—no band in the school would let him sit in—so during lunchtime, he would go to the track field and just walk around by himself playing harmonica. The harmonica is "one of those things that everybody can play," he explains. "If you have the right key harmonica that matches the song, there's no way you can play a wrong note, so you can fake it pretty well." But to make it a real craft, "to be able to play melodies and be expressive," he told me, you have to play all the time—"you have to eat and sleep it."

One night at the Rubaiyat club in Dallas, Mickey met his hero Donnie Brooks—and the harmonica legend taught Mickey a few licks. Those five minutes with Donnie gave Mickey the idea that he could make a go at a career. His commitment soon paid off. He started hanging out at his neighborhood's recording studio, dropping into sessions—from jingles to full albums—that could use a harmonica lick. And one night at a party, Willie Nelson heard Mickey play and asked him to sit in with his band on a recording session sometime. Soon enough, Nelson asked Mickey to *join* the band—and Mickey's been touring with Willie ever since. Their decades of traveling together have brought Mickey all around the world. He's even played for a president or two.

For artisans, it's not just honing their craft that makes up the long haul—it's also performing the craft after gaining expertise. Some artisans are remembered for their magnum opus—their one "great work" to which everything was building. More often, great artisans are remembered for their corpus—their whole body of work. Since before I can remember, I have been entranced by late-night talk show hosts, like David Letterman. Letterman would do mostly the same run of show, over and over again—and no particular show would stand out that much. But there would be an atmosphere created by how he did every show—and that atmosphere was his "great work." You see the same with auteur filmmakers who commit to a distinctive visual style, bands that commit to a distinctive sound, or chefs who commit to a distinctive flavor. Each of these artisans might have some magnum opus you can point to that captures their style, but it's their corpus—their whole body of work—that we steep in. Willa Cather put it well: An artist "tries to present the experiences and emotions of a group of people by the light of his own." When we fall in love with some artisan's body of work, what we love is their consistent "light"—how it bounces off the latest thing in front of them.

Companions

The most important commitment of all is commitment to other people. This is the work of *companions*. It's a beautiful word: With *com-* meaning "with" and *pan-* meaning "bread," a companion is "one who breaks bread with another." To be a companion to someone is to *accompany* them in life—to be present, together. What more do we want in life than to accompany and be accompanied?

It reminds me of something Pope Francis once said about how he wanted the Catholic Church to be like a "field hospital":

> The thing the church needs most today is the ability to heal wounds and to warm the hearts of the faithful; it needs nearness, proximity. I see the church as a field hospital after battle. It is useless to ask a seriously injured person if he has high cholesterol and about the level of his blood sugars! You have to heal his wounds. Then we can talk about everything else. Heal the wounds, heal the wounds.

Companions are the people who are present with us after the battles of life.

I think about teachers, who are at their best not when they're educational performers, but rather when they are simply accompanying students through the learning process. Georgia teacher Tamaiko Chappell sees her work as showing students that they are on a long journey to understand math—and that she'll be with them along the way. She gets students to see that "no problem is unsolvable"—and then sees them through the process. The process of learning math, she explains, is filled with frustration at every level. There's a lot of trial and error. The art of Tamaiko's work is getting kids to not quit—to face down problems with the solace of knowing "there's always someone here to help you if you're stuck."

But becoming a trusted companion isn't quick or easy. Jason Slattery, who directs a mentoring program at the DC Dream Center that pairs adults with kids in need of mentorship, told me that new volunteer mentors often "want to have an intimate close relationship right at the drop of a hat" but are frustrated to find that mentorship doesn't work that way. "To really earn the trust and to really know your child and for them to really know you," the center's director Ernest Clover explained, takes three years. A mentor needs to keep showing up, because kids need to hear "I choose you" over and over again in order to trust them. Often, Jason says, the least charismatic volunteers end up being the best mentors, because the critical factor in mentorship is not charm but dedication.

The same is true in religious life. Joseph Phillips, the lead pastor at the Neighborhood Church in Charlotte, North Carolina, takes seriously the meaning of *pastor*. He believes that in huge congregations, where the minister can't possibly remember everyone's names, the pastor might be able to teach people but won't really be able to pastor to them. Pastoring, in Joseph's view, is relentlessly specific. It's about connecting faith to the actual, particular people in a congregation. It's knowing which families are struggling—and taking time to be present with them through their particular challenges.

"There are so few people that have any real relationships that they can reach to when there's a crisis," he reminds his fellow pastors.

Joseph sees his calling as sitting with the tension of having "that level of intimacy with people": "Everything's exposed, everything's laid bare, and here you are holding all of that, making space for all of that, and just listening."

Teacher-student, mentor-mentee, and pastor-congregant relationships are formal examples of companionship, but most of the companionship in our lives is more informal. There's an old-fashioned phrase "kith and kin," meaning "friends and relatives." You can still hear some people talk about their "kin" these days, but the idea of one's "kith"—one's good neighbors and old friends—has fallen by the wayside. But it's a commitment to being faithful "kith" that weaves communities together.

The writer Gracy Olmstead talks often about her hometown in Idaho, where neighbors lived together for generations. It was a place where, in her words, "your last name meant more than your first," because your neighbors weren't just neighbors—they were also people who knew your great-grandparents. This stability—and these multigenerational ties—led the whole town to watch over one another.

Gracy only started noticing the power of "kith" in her hometown when she moved away. Neighbors in her new community don't watch over one another in the same way—they often don't even know one another. When she started understanding this contrast, she wanted to let the world know more about what her hometown could teach the rest of us. But what do the rest of us do? If we don't live in a town or neighborhood like the one where she grew up—if we never have—do we just give up?

Gracy once read that a good friend doesn't need to be someone you get along with perfectly or who has everything in common with you; they just need to be someone who's "built up the skill of being a good friend" over time. She thinks of being a good neighbor the same way.

"You don't necessarily have to be surrounded by people who are good at it or who have lots in common with you," she said. "But by practicing the art of being a good neighbor, you'll pull out those skills in the people around you and hopefully, over time, foster the sorts of ingredients that will inspire other good neighbors." In other words, friendliness and neighborliness are contagious.

Gracy's parents host Friday night pizza nights, where anyone is welcome. At the beginning, only their own kids came. But over time, their kids brought friends. Eventually the neighbors found out about the open invitation. Now pizza night is frequented "by all sorts of people." And her parents now have visitors *every* day of the week—people "stop by their house constantly for a word of advice or for a quick cup of tea or emotional support." Their tiny commitment to open their home on Friday night has made everyone feel like their home is a welcoming one.

Whenever someone questions whether commitment in today's culture is possible, I think about parents. We take for granted the act of parenthood because it is common, but it's really an amazing phenomenon. When we choose to have children, we are committing to a lifetime of care—and about twenty years of deeply engaged care—for something outside ourselves. Despite all the talk of widespread hopelessness about the coming decades, our choice to have kids belies our despair. When we have children, we are committing to the future.

Perhaps even more remarkable than our commitment to our children—whom we are wired to commit to, after all—is the continued power of marriage. For all the browsing that liquid modernity brings, marriage remains. You can tell that having kids and getting married remain the last, lingering commitments of the modern age because we use them to describe other commitments we care about deeply. It's why you hear people say, "I'm married to the shop," or "This project is my baby." Wendell Berry has even said that a proliferation of "marriages"—not just to spouses, but to all causes and places needing connection and commitment—is the way we should think about what will heal the world. The giving of one's word; the facing of the unknown that comes with giving up some control; accepting certain limits; understanding that every single thing that comes with the bond may not make us happy, but the bond, as a whole, will—all are present in marriage and in other commitments, too.

Berry laments that we live in the age of divorce—not just in terms of literal marriages, but in terms of the breaking of all sorts of commitments. We cannot individually put it all back together again. But "what you do," Berry recommends, "is the only thing that you can do": "You take two things that ought to be together and you put them back together. Two things, not all things. That's the way the work has to go."

This is the call of the Counterculture of Commitment: to do one's part in making our too-often-dissected, too-often-isolated, too-often-divorced world a bit more whole.

7

The Fear of Regret and the Freedom of Purpose

At the beginning of a commitment journey, we're often gripped by the fear of regret: the fear that if we commit to something, we will later regret having not committed to something else instead. We don't want to wake up twenty years down the line haunted by what could have been if we chose something else. It's natural to feel pain when making decisions. The *-cide* in *decide*, after all, is the same as in *homicide*. It means "to cut" or "to strike"—to separate from something; to keep one part and leave the rest. When we are young, the philosopher Roberto Unger writes, we are "a storehouse of alternative ways of becoming a person." But we can't be everything. Choosing a path is "indispensable to our self-development," but it's also "a mutilation," for "in choosing, as we must, we cast aside many aspects of our humanity." This is why we can feel such a strong fear of regret. If we're going to go through this agonizing process of becoming something instead of everything, it is crucial for us to pick right.

Lowering the stakes

Overcoming the fear of regret starts with lowering the stakes. It helps to remember that not every commitment is an existential saga, and that not all commitments have to be permanent. Commitments are relationships, and relationships are like living things. And living things die. When the life has gone out of a commitment, it's no longer a relationship—it's just a dead rule. It's good to take on relationships and invest in them, and it's good to work to heal relationships when they are sick. But when they are dead, they are dead. And there's something morbid about playacting what's not there anymore.

Praising quitting may seem strange in a book about making commitments. But being okay with the idea that things might not work out is key to dedication, because it helps us lower the stakes of taking on new commitments in the first place. A long-haul hero in Baltimore, Max Pollock, cofounded an organization that salvages and resells bricks and wood from around the city. These days, Max doesn't think much about his commitment to his project, Brick + Board, at all. "I don't wake up each morning taking this vow of commitment to my work," he says. "It just feels like this is what I want to be doing and I will give it everything I have. I never question whether or not this is what I want." This is what a living commitment, at its most alive, feels like: hardly anything at all. It's just a part of you.

But Max only got there by quitting something else. A few years ago, he was six weeks into law school. One day he was walking around West Philadelphia with his girlfriend when he saw some guys fixing up an old house.

"Gosh, I don't want to be in law school," he told her. "I want to be doing what they're doing."

To his surprise, she responded: "Well, do it, then!"

Max remembers thinking, *It's really that simple—I just stop doing the thing that I don't want to be doing and start doing the thing I do want to be doing.* A few days later, he dropped out of school and started working at a design and build firm that did salvage work around the city. Max didn't quit school because it was hard—because boredom, distraction, or uncertainty got the best of him. He quit because it was no longer a living commitment. Comfort with quitting is not just okay—it's part of being a long-haul hero. And knowing this can ease your nerves when you're facing down a hard decision.

Making choices and taking steps

Once you've lowered the stakes, you still have to make a choice. And choosing from multiple options can be tough—even paralyzing. In my discussions with long-haul heroes, I have encountered a few helpful methods for breaking this paralysis. One method is to enlist the help of our emotions. My friend Jon has a goofy but effective way of doing this. When people ask him advice, instead of weighing different options with them in the abstract, he just tells them what they should do. If they ask, "Should I take the job in Philadelphia or Atlanta?" he responds, "Definitely Atlanta—do it."

When Jon does this, people are usually surprised, because that's not how these conversations usually go. Most advice-givers join advice-seekers in their indecision: "*Well, okay, here are the pros and cons of Atlanta.*" But Jon's method often works because it forces people to imagine themselves actually taking one of the options. Once he says "definitely Atlanta" to someone, the prospect of living in Atlanta becomes more real to them—and their emotions come out. The grappler might say, "I just can't see myself living there—it doesn't feel right." Then Jon responds: "There you go—Philadelphia it is."

The geneticist Susan Wessler advises students grappling with career paths to ask themselves, "What's the thing on your to-do list that you always want to do first?" All the cold analysis in the world about what we want is no match for just noticing what, in daily life, enlivens us—and what doesn't.

Enlisting emotions is also key to another method of making decisions: the centuries-old Jesuit practice of Ignatian discernment. Practitioners clear their mind, deeply envision different options one by one, and then feel for movements within as they envision each option. They're not supposed to only *think* about the advantages and disadvantages of the options—they're supposed to *feel* them. The practice is more than just an examination of options—it's an examination of yourself having been presented with those options. Or as St. Ignatius put it five centuries ago: "Much light and understanding are derived through experience of desolations and consolations and discernment of diverse spirits."

The question practitioners ask themselves is: As I imagine myself taking this option, do I feel support, encouragement, or peace of mind (in the Jesuits' belief, closer to God)—or do I feel guilt, anxiety, or distance from the divine?

One Jesuit I interviewed says the practice is, at its core, about "attunement." Our feelings have access to information that our rational mind does not, and to practice Ignatian discernment is to try to tune our internal receivers to better hear that information.

It's visceral, wrote the Jesuit priest James Keenan. You don't just search your head or even your heart. "You search your guts."

In addition to enlisting our feelings to help make decisions, we can also enlist our values. But this can be hard, for many of us struggle to identify and articulate what we believe in. One way I have discovered my values is by collecting heroes. I try to learn about different peoples' lives, see which ones inspire me, and then learn what I can about the ones who do. And here's what's great about really getting to know how your heroes think and act: When faced with a hard decision, you can reflect on what they might have chosen if faced with a similar one. They're our heroes because they share our values. In asking which options, if taken, would make your heroes proud, you're asking which options align with your deepest beliefs.

If the first decision-making method was about enlisting your guts, and the second was about enlisting your heart, a final method—rational analysis—is about enlisting your mind. The textbook tool of rational decision-making is the "pro and con list." It was actually Ben Franklin who made the first modern mention of one, writing in a 1772 letter to the chemist Joseph Priestley:

> ". . . my Way is, to divide half a Sheet of Paper by a Line into two Columns, writing over the one Pro, and over the other Con. Then during three or four Days Consideration I put down under the different Heads short Hints of the different Motives that at different Times occur to me for or against the Measure . . . And tho' the Weight of Reasons cannot be taken with the Precision of Algebraic Quantities, yet when each is thus considered separately and comparatively, and the whole lies before me, I think I can judge better, and am less likely to take a rash Step; and in fact I have found great Advantage from this kind of Equation, in what may be called Moral or Prudential Algebra."

In daily life, our technology for "Moral or Prudential algebra" hasn't advanced much in the centuries since Franklin's era. To rationally analyze decisions today, our best bet is still to do as he did: to break down our options into their constituent parts and analyze them piece by piece.

Big decisions might require enlisting not just one method, but all three—emotions, values, and rationality. These methods are usually only, to use the writer Parker Palmer's word, "an exoskeleton" for our decisions: scaffolding to orient us toward the place we should be looking. In the end, what we are waiting for is that spark of life that makes a choice feel right. It's a mix of positive emotions, inspiration, and a sense of reasonableness that will lead us one way or another.

Most decision-making methods have one thing in common: quieting the outside noise to listen for answers. Think of Blaise Pascal's observation: "All of humanity's problems stem from man's inability to sit quietly in a room alone." Or as the songwriter Joe Pug sings, a little more bluntly, "If you shut up with what you've chosen, you'll hear something choosing you."

But once you do, you can't just sit there. If you do, the fear of regret will creep back in. We can only fully learn what we want when we take action. This is the insight of "Dive in and find out," or "Just do it."

When I asked long-haul heroes what made them able to dive into a commitment, many cited their comfort with the unknown. For Andy Shallal, the founder of DC's Busboys and Poets restaurants, not knowing what was on the other side of his choice to open a restaurant was part of the excitement. Shallal didn't stress about the entire journey when he made his commitment. He just thought about the first steps. "I don't take ten-year journeys," he explained. "I take one-step-at-a-time journeys."

He didn't meticulously plan every single detail of what the restaurant would look like—he just had sketches of ideas. He wanted it to be a big space, so people could have meetings and events there. He wanted it to be a place where people could be educated, enlightened, and exposed to new ideas. He wanted it to feel like a part of DC—a cultural center for the city. But he did not flesh these ideas out all at once. He realized them, piece by piece, as they came up. Soon, his one-step-at-a-time journey became a fifteen-year long haul toward perhaps the most beloved chain of restaurants and community gathering spaces in the nation's capital.

Kimberly Wasserman, who spent twelve years fighting to shut down toxic coal power plants in her Chicago neighborhood, said she never really thought about herself embarking on a yearslong struggle. She just thought "something had to be done, no matter how long it took." Her work was day by day.

"Every day was a new day to take them on," she said. "Every day was another day to work to shut them down."

Every time she drove by the plant with her son, whose lungs had been poisoned by the plant's fumes, he would ask, "Mom, did you shut them down today?"

Responding "No, not yet" made her feel even more determined. She never thought about quitting, but never really thought, *Oh, we're getting closer*, either. She just kept thinking, *What do we have to do today to get what we need in our neighborhood?*

Ryan Gravel, the visionary behind Atlanta's BeltLine, told me that he's "a fan of naiveté." If he had known how much work it would take to convert Atlanta's old railway lines into a major multiuse trail—let alone how much drama it would bring to his life—he might not have gone through with it. But "naiveté is really powerful," he insists. Because he didn't know it at the beginning, he committed to his big idea and, step by step, he followed through. Looking back, knowing what he knows now, he has no regrets about embarking on the project.

This theme popped up again and again in my conversations with long-haul heroes: Grand commitments do not need grand blueprints. Grand blueprints mean more things to poke holes in, more things that can disappoint, and more reasons not to commit. As the Yiddish proverb goes: "Man plans, and God laughs." What grand commitments start with are first steps. You know your first step, get comfortable with the uncertainty about what comes next, and then you go for it.

Some people think that when we're picking between options, what we're trying to do is pick the option that gets closest to some perfect future. Choosing, in this view, is a quiz with a right answer. But that can't be right, because the future doesn't already exist. Our choices create the future. Our reality becomes whatever we commit to.

The challenge of choosing is less about picking the "right" future and more about what to do with the future we inevitably pick. As the Stanford Graduate School of Business lecturer Ed Batista puts it, we should focus less on making the right decisions, and more on making sure our decisions *turn out right*. Fellow Stanford professor Baba Shiv, who studies the neuroscience of decision-making, makes a similar point: The major factor for successful decisions is not what option decision-makers choose, but whether the decision-makers remain committed to their choice.

One of my high school teachers once gave us romance advice that echoes Batista's and Shiv's findings. He told us that we should give up on the idea that our partners should be "the one"—the perfect soul mate with whom we were destined to be. When you start to think someone's "the one," you constantly compare them to some perfect, abstract "one" in your head. When you think this way, he explained, every problem that arises in your relationship could be taken as evidence that the person just isn't the one. Instead, he told us, we should focus on the fact that we have committed to a partnership—and work on making that partnership work. Rather than thinking back to the original decision to form the partnership when things get hard, we can remind ourselves: "This is part of the work of tending to a commitment."

Commitments are not defined by whether the singular moment in the past, when they were created, was "right." Commitments are better thought of as "thriving" or "languishing." It's true that an initial choice will affect a commitment's prospects for thriving or languishing. But over time, a commitment's vitality is determined not by one moment, but every moment along the way.

Knowing what your guts, heart, and head are telling you; taking action in the face of uncertainty; and giving up on the idea of a perfect future—it's all easier to talk about than to do. All the advice in the world doesn't change the fact that a commitment is an exercise in faith. In order to do it, we need to believe in the naturalist John Burroughs's advice: "Leap, and the net will appear." But even that might be more than we need to hear. Often, all we need to hear when on the brink of a commitment is: *Leap!*

Commitment's momentum

Once you've made a decision and started to act on it, the option you've chosen will become very real very quickly. Worries about all that comes with your newfound commitment—the burdens you might have to carry, the people you might have to meet, the lines you might have to toe—start flooding in. You start internalizing all the time and energy that is going to be given to the commitment—and, in turn, notice all the other opportunities slipping away. Before you made the decision, its potential consequences were abstract. Now that they're concrete, the fear of regret may come creeping in again.

You may have experienced this feeling in *literal* Infinite Browsing Mode. You overcome the anxiety of picking a movie, but now, as the opening credits start to roll, you feel that pang of regret again. Perhaps you start thinking, "Do I really want to spend the next two hours watching this?" And when the exit button is still in sight, a voice in your head shouts: *Pick something else!*

The only way out is powering through. But here's the good news: At a certain point—and it comes not that far into a commitment—the commitment picks up its own momentum. It's like that moment a couple of minutes into a movie, where you stop thinking, *Should I keep watching this movie?*, and start just enjoying it. The commitment takes on a life of its own—and requires much less will to sustain.

Leslie Merriman is a librarian in my hometown. Ten years ago, she became interested in Middle Eastern history and politics. She learned about the Arab Spring and Syrian Civil War on the news and started devouring all the information she could find. Moved by what she'd learned, she started donating to the Red Crescent and Syrian American Medical Society, but kept feeling like there was more she could do. When she heard about a local organization helping Afghan refugees settle in the United States, she reached out to get involved.

The group was understaffed and the coordinator was happy that someone signed up to help. She told Leslie that the group had hundreds of refugee families around the area, and no one to check in on them. Would she help?

"Sure," Leslie said. "Just send me some info." But when she received back a list of a hundred families to check in on, Leslie learned she was one of the group's *only* volunteers in the DC area. She wasn't given much guidance except to call the families and see if there was anything she or the organization could do to help with the transition to American life.

Leslie started calling down the list, family by family, asking how they were and what they needed.

"I love the unknown," she said, echoing a theme of many committers. "So not knowing what this person could ask of me was very intriguing." And she felt like she was putting her librarian skills to use. "I'm good at research, so I don't need to promise I can provide everything," she said. "I can just help find the answer."

The requests piled up. Someone was in a one-bedroom apartment with their family of eight, their wife was sick, and they needed a job. Someone's kid had disabilities and needed services. Someone's family was running out of diapers, and another family needed jackets. Everyone needed help learning English.

Leslie did what she could. She would drive people to the doctor, run diaper and jacket drives, talk families through crises, connect children with grief counselors, and sign parents up for English classes. Often she would just visit and listen—a friendly welcome wagon in a strange new country.

Leslie eventually brought others into her commitment. She would call up her dentist friend and beg him to give free dental work to families. She would call up her psychiatrist friend and ask for referrals. She would post on Facebook to get necessary answers and procure donated goods. She even talked to her own kids about sharing their toys and clothes with the families she was helping.

Over just a few months, Leslie's whole life changed. Her fridge filled up with Afghan food—thank-you gifts for all her help. She soon had more Afghan friends than family members at her holiday dinners. She started feeling like she was managing a little empire of aid—triaging different situations, scrapping and thrifting donations and volunteers, and deputizing people she had already helped in order to help out new people in need.

Leslie can't go back to her old way of life, and she wouldn't want to. She gets a little annoyed when her friends complain about late Amazon orders or feel depressed about "not having much going on." Once your priorities shift and you have important work to do, she explains, "the little mundane crap" of daily life—problems with your job or manager or dog or partner—fade to the background. Commitment has its own momentum.

And it's not just extraordinary commitments like Leslie's that take on a life of their own. One day, shortly after she had retired, my mom passed a booth in downtown DC recruiting volunteers for Miriam's Kitchen, an advocacy and service center for people experiencing homelessness. She signed up for one shift. Suddenly that one shift became a weekly shift; soon after that, it was a twice-weekly shift. After volunteering for a while, coordinators there asked my mom if she had any other skills she could share with center guests, so she started teaching knitting classes. She soon started inviting others to come volunteer, too. In a few months, that one shift had snowballed into a major part of her life.

There's an organization, Better Block, that encourages you to just pick a block in your town and commit to making it better. It's as simple as it sounds: You analyze a block and do everything you can do—formally and informally—to improve it. It started when two friends in Dallas—Jason Roberts and Andrew Howard—decided to pick a four-block area and see how much they could do to improve it in twenty-four hours. In the course of a day, they added bike lanes, temporary awnings, and café tables. They used potted plants to build a makeshift median. They invited local artists and food vendors to set up shop in front of abandoned storefronts. After everyone saw how much a little commitment could do, the whole block transformed. Vacancy rates plummeted. Active storefronts nearly tripled. Now Jason travels the country encouraging others to do the same. Some call it 'urban acupuncture'—making tiny, loving interventions that start the process of transforming a nondescript space into a beloved place.

By focusing participants' attention on one tiny corner of a city—literally one block—Better Block keeps people from feeling overwhelmed. Problems can seem immense, but Roberts encourages us to just get started.

"If you went ahead and started implementing one thing that's going to take you two months, that's going to make it a little better," he said. "And then if you work on another thing that's going to take another two months, that will make it a little better still. And in no time—within a year—you are going to look back and think, *Wow, we've made some pretty dramatic change to this space.*"

Commitments have their own momentum for two reasons. First, the more we commit to something, the more it opens up to us. As outsiders, we can only see and understand a slice of what that thing might be. But when we're in the room, in the relationship, or in the community, we start to see it all—and that is a rush. When you commit to a neighborhood, new people, places, and events come into your life. When you join up with a cause, you learn an epic story of enemies, heroes, and challenges. All this is a lot like personal relationships: You start out intrigued from afar. But as you enter deeper into the relationship, you start falling in love.

Commitment also has its own momentum because we psychologically adapt to the commitment we make. We have a "psychological immune system": Our brain puts in extra work to make us feel pleased with our circumstances. When researchers ask people how they would feel if they won the lottery, they guess that they would be tremendously happy. When they ask people how they would feel if they lost their legs in an accident, they guess that they would be tremendously sad. But when researchers interview actual lottery winners and accident victims a few years after their life-changing events, they don't feel *that* much different than they did before. Everyone overestimates the psychological effects of change, because we underestimate the power of our psychological immune system.

Our psychological immune system works by weaving new stories out of our new circumstances. We start finding less meaning in what's outside of our control and new meaning in what's within our control. We psychologically adapt to our past decisions, rationalizing why we made them rather than agonizing over whether we made them *correctly*.

But this feature only works when we really lock in our decisions. Harvard's Daniel Gilbert, who studies the psychological immune system, found that these positive psychological adaptations are short-circuited if it's too easy to go back on the decision. In one study, Gilbert asked photography students to take two meaningful photos.

He then had them print out the two and invited them to keep one and discard the other. He told half the group that the decision was final. He told the other half that they could change their mind later. A few days later, he asked the students about how satisfied they were with the photo they chose. The students who could not change their mind were much more satisfied with the photos they chose than the ones who could. Changeable outcomes, Gilbert's findings suggest, are less satisfying than unchangeable ones.

Amy Jones works in the industry that could aptly be called "the commitment business": She's a tattoo artist. She remembers the exact moment, fifteen years ago, when she knew she would stay in her line of work for the long haul. She was having trouble deciding whether she wanted to keep her tattoo skills recreational or if she wanted to get serious and go professional. One day, she said to herself, "You know what? I'm going to go all in." She got a face tattoo.

It was her way of making her decision less changeable. "Once you tattoo your face," she said, "you're kind of getting out of the, you know, white-collar world. It's not like I'm ever going to be a Walmart greeter now."

Getting the face tattoo put Amy's mind at ease, because there was no going back on being a tattoo artist and therefore no more questioning.

"There's no on-the fence-moment," she says. "You're just on this side now and you just gotta do it and give your one hundred percent to be what you want in this business."

You don't have to get a face tattoo like Amy to have your psychological immune system kick in and ease your mind. But a proverbial face tattoo—something that makes your decision a little less changeable—will help.

Conversion

In many ways, every commitment journey is a long conversion—a rewiring of your sense of meaning in the world. Religious commitments, of course, convert you, in the popular sense of the term. But so do political ones. People talk about their life before and after feminism, before and after anti-racism, and before and after unionizing their workplace. A place can also convert you, which you can see when people describe themselves as having "become a true New Yorker" or "true Texan." Love is one big conversion: To see your life as one with your partner in it, or with your child in it, transforms you. So it is with all commitments. In some ways, we become a different person every time we truly commit to anyone or anything.

When my friend Liz became a mom, her whole sense of meaning was rearranged. A new coat of paint, for example, meant more when it would cover the walls of "a home I was building my family in." What she once thought mattered all of a sudden didn't.

"I would rather be home with my babies on a Friday night than going out," she explained. For her, becoming a mom is her greatest accomplishment. All the hardships of her parenthood journey are subsumed by the meaning it brings.

"It's funny," she said. "You're so tired and can't wait for your kids to go to bed at night, but then you sit there and you stare at them thinking, *Oh, my gosh, they're so perfect, they're so beautiful. Look at them!*"

It makes sense that fire is the common metaphor for conversion. Think about lighting a match: It starts tiny, sparked through a bit of tension—and then it spreads and takes over. The death penalty abolitionist Sister Helen Prejean says she wakes up every morning and prays not for understanding, but to catch on fire. That's what a commitment that has taken hold of you feels like. It is alive, it is invigorating, it is comforting, it is sometimes treacherous, and—most significantly—it fills up the space.

Once the fire has taken hold, the final step in a commitment journey is to lock it in by vocalizing your commitment swiftly and openly. All cultures have ceremonies to help us with the process of vocalizing new commitments to others—of "locking in" our conversion. Think of housewarming parties where people come together to welcome you to a new place. Professions have oaths to declare yourself bound by the ethics of the craft. Perhaps the most common ceremony of this type is a wedding, where you vocalize your commitment to your life partner in front of your community.

There are informal ceremonies of commitment, too. Twelve-step programs have initiations where members declare their sobriety. Evangelical churches use altar calls for congregants to vocalize their beliefs to the congregation. Amy, the tattoo artist, tells me that many of her clients experience their tattooings as rituals of "locking in" and vocalizing commitments. She sometimes even feels like a pastor. "It's a very moving moment to alter someone's body for the rest of their life," she tells me. "I respect that space."

At the end of this whole process—of choosing, of diving in, of converting, and of vocalizing to others—your commitment is imprinted on your identity. Usually, this is where any lingering fears of regret dissipate. You're no longer picking a commitment that lives outside of you and seeing if it fits. Instead, you're bringing the commitment inside—into relationship with you—so that it becomes part of your identity. The fears fade away, because you're not really making a choice anymore. Your commitment has become part of who you are.

Vocation

Another way of putting this journey is that it is the process of realizing your "vocation"—of listening for a calling and then enacting it. The Quakers have a phrase for this: "Let your life speak." First, as writer Parker Palmer explains, you hear from within what you are meant to be. And then, in responding to what you heard, you tell the world about your calling.

Father Brian McDermott, who has been a Jesuit priest for over half a century, describes feeling, during the period when he committed to being a priest, like he was being "claimed by someone."

There were "no high mystical moments," he said, "just a steady undertow of being drawn" to church life. When asked about how he "puts in the work" of sustaining his commitment year after year, he challenges the premise.

"I would be gone long ago if it was about my will," he said. Commitment is not about gripping hold with all your strength—it's a relationship.

"God has his talons in me," Father McDermott said with a smile. That's what a calling feels like—something that steadily pulls you and then has a hold on you.

To have a sense of vocation adds a certain sanctity to our commitments. It is to see our commitments not as random choices we make, but as callings that emanate from a deeper place. Vocations make us comfortable with our limits and less haunted by unchosen options, because they come from an inner voice that tells us it is all right that we are not everything. When you have a sense of vocation, you know that the way you can be most helpful is by playing the part you are called to play well.

Finding a vocation is like being assigned an instrument in a cosmic orchestra. Your calling joins with others to perform something beautiful. It's a form of belonging—to let your life speak is to join with all the others who are doing the same. This is part of why we can think of committers as making up a counterculture. When you love a particular place, you join with all the other patriots who love their particular places, which together adds up to the whole world being loved. When you love particular people, you join with all the other companions loving their particular people, which together adds up to the whole of humanity being loved. When you build something, you are participating in the world's reconstruction project. When you steward something, you are participating in the world's maintenance.

This is the view that our lives count for something—that we have a purpose. And as we pursue our purpose—as we honor our calling—we stay close to that deep, inner voice that originally spoke to us. This sense of purpose is the gift on the other side of the fear of regret.

It's a gift because it liberates us from ourselves. Young people are often accused of being self-centered or even narcissistic. We're told to "get over" ourselves. But this is a misunderstanding of how narcissism works. It actually works like this: When we are born, we need to be built up—we need self-esteem—to get going in life. While that's happening, we risk being separated into two pieces—our true self inside and our outer shell. Narcissism takes root when we build up the shell instead of the actual self. The result is that we don't tend to our inner self, and the outer self sucks up all the growth. Narcissists are weak people surrounded by a puffed-up shell.

Being narcissistic doesn't feel good. You know you're weak inside, but you're afraid of getting found out. And when your puffed-out shell is pierced, you're destroyed. This cycle is vicious, because as you get weaker and weaker, and more and more scared, you keep frantically bolstering the shell to protect yourself. Narcissism is not an obsession with oneself. It's an obsession with one's shell.

But you can't defeat narcissism with finger-wagging. The call to "get out of yourself" reminds me of what my doctor once told me when I was trying to quit drinking Coke: "Don't tell yourself, 'Drink less Coke.' Tell yourself: 'Drink more water.'" Alternatives to bad situations are always better than admonishments. If young people are narcissistic, it doesn't help to tell us to "be less selfish." We need alternatives.

That's what commitments are—alternatives to self-obsession. Commitments free us to dedicate ourselves to something bigger than ourselves—to something beyond our shells. The French philosopher Jacques Maritain said that the meaning of life is "self-mastery for the purpose of self-giving." This is the challenge of growing up—to turn the corner from self-mastery to self-giving. What is the moment at that corner—between inwardness, growth, and concerted self-development and outwardness, public interestedness, and other-centeredness? Commitment.

When you have purpose, you can be proactive rather than reactive. You can focus on your inner values rather than outer ones, which often distract. You are given the types of responsibilities that everybody pines for: You can become a producer rather than just a consumer; you can become a person in relationship to the world rather than someone just using it. People who commit often discover that selfishness is not ambitious enough—that their purpose gives them the types of challenges that so many talk about wanting to have, the "strenuous life" that so many talk about wanting to lead.

And as we pursue our purpose, we get stronger. We learn new skills to live up to our commitments. We conquer fears that we never would have conquered otherwise. We cultivate our inner self through fulfilling our commitments. The outer shell that comes with narcissism is faux, brittle solidity. Commitment leads to strong, organic solidity. It's solid like a tree trunk, not like a wall.

When we're young, we often want freedom *from* the world. We want an unencumbered self, where nothing outside touches us and where we have no responsibility or rules. This is a limited freedom—it's, to use Alasdair MacIntyre's phrase, the "freedom of ghosts." Purpose gives us freedom *in* the world. It's the freedom that comes when we enter into relationship with particular parts of the world—when we develop an ability to respond to them, and therefore feel a responsibility *for* them. When we fulfill that responsibility, we get to experience real pride. Commitment is co-owning a little part of existence and, in doing so, loving existence itself a little bit more.

This freedom of purpose is much deeper than the freedom of ghosts. My neighbor Christopher Fay has a good way of putting it: Through commitment, he explains, "you are demonstrating to yourself that you are someone of substance." Through commitment, "you become real to yourself."

What a funny quirk of being: It is only in turning away from ourselves that we can discover who we are.

8

The Fear of Association and the Comfort of Friends

Commitment often involves other people's rules, other people's needs, other people's problems, and other people's way of doing things. Attaching to something larger than ourselves brings messiness, anxiety, and discomfort. This leads to another fear that can hold us back from commitment: *the fear of association*. It's the fear that dedication will threaten our identity, reputation, and sense of control.

Identity, reputation, and control

When we associate with something, we risk becoming more like it. This is a threat to our sense of identity. We ask ourselves, worryingly, "Am I *really* the type of person who does this?" To take on a new commitment, we need to overcome our preexisting self-conceptions.

When someone says they don't want to get married because they are "not a relationship person," part of what they're saying is that a committed relationship threatens their identity. When someone doesn't want to join up with a cause because they don't want to think of themself as "political," part of what they're saying is that being openly political threatens their identity. Union organizers often talk of running into workers who worry about joining a union because they do not see themself as the "type of worker who complains."

The Pennsylvania community organizer Jonathan Smucker has noticed something funny about association and identity. He writes that the most contentious internal battle inside any new activist group is often the writing of the group's mission statement, because it implicates members' identities much more than other parts of building the organization. When something becomes about how a group's members "conceived of ourselves and projected our identities," he writes, compromise became difficult.

If identity threat is about how our commitments can threaten how we see *ourselves*, reputation threat is about how our commitments can threaten how *others* see us. Jean-Paul Sartre famously wrote that "Hell is other people." The quote is often thought to mean that it's a shame we have to put up with other people—it's best to be alone. But what Sartre specifically meant by the phrase was that the presence of other people brings judgment into our lives.

"By the mere appearance of the Other," Sartre wrote, "I am put in the position of passing judgment on myself as on an object, for it is as an object that I appear to the Other." The "other people" are "hell" because they cause us to judge ourselves through their eyes.

This is reputation threat—fear of other people's judgment. We fear that when we commit to something and other people know about it, we lose control over our public image. Reputation threat is at work when you do not support a candidate publicly because you worry others will scoff. It's at work when you do not want to join a religion because it means you are accountable, in the eyes of others, for its flaws. It's at work when you worry about dating someone because of what being with them says to your friends about who you are. The writer Casper ter Kuile argues that reputation threat is why so many young people don't connect with institutions. "It's very, very hard for people, once they are unaffiliated, to commit to an institution today," he explains. "They feel like they would have to defend the whole institution: its history, its politics, its inevitable failings."

Commitments that involve others also threaten our sense of control—over our time, over our energy, and over our decision-making. When we associate with something, we have to deal with the full chaos that comes with it. You associate with something because you like parts of it, but nobody likes *all* the parts of it. Much of what we can associate with—causes, institutions, communities, people—is messy. There are few cafeteria relationships, where you take what you like about a person or organization and leave what you don't. Friends have ups and downs. Spouses have traits that grate on you. Causes have internal strife. Communities are filled with various types of people, many of whom are difficult. If you're going to start a band, you're going to need to find someone to play every instrument; if you're going to start a restaurant, you're going to need to go to city hall. And most everything involves lots of boring meetings.

Sometimes it's not the messiness but the orderliness that can come with a new commitment that threatens our sense of control. Institutions have rituals, ceremonies, practices, and norms, many of which are annoying. Crafts have formats you have to follow, especially at first. Causes have times when you need to "take one for the team." You join a religion because you like most of what it's about, but there are some parts of it that don't sit well with you. You exert your will to choose something bigger than yourself at the outset of a commitment, but because it is bigger than yourself, what it eventually asks of you is also bigger than your original choice. You are left asking: "I am okay with submitting to part of this, but do I want to submit to *all* of this?"

Association also forces us to reveal more of ourselves than we thought we wanted. To commit alongside other people, we have to reveal ourselves—our weaknesses, strengths, capabilities, and interests. The longer we associate, the more we reveal. In the long run, we are all together in the truth about who we are. This requires a whole lot of vulnerability. It's what the essayist Tim Kreider meant when he wrote that "if we want the rewards of being loved, we have to submit to the mortifying ordeal of being known."

Two views of the self

To overcome the fear of association, we need to change the way we think about ourselves. Our fears about threats to our identity, reputation, and sense of control come from a view of the self as something that is static and isolated. In this view, we have a series of locked-in personal qualities: "I love sushi, my favorite band is the Rolling Stones, I cheer for the Lakers, I'm an electrician." It's like a dating profile or Facebook page: You have your preferences, and your task in life is to find the people and products that work with and satisfy them.

If you believe that you have a static and isolated self, everything that doesn't mesh well with you is a threat. You're going to have anxiety about making choices that best align with your "true self." But there is no perfect match. There is no cause, place, community, craft, profession—and definitely no person—that will line up perfectly with all your current qualities.

But there's an alternate view of the self that better allows for commitment. It's to see the self not as static but dynamic; not as rigid but organic. In this view, our identity is not fixed but built through our relationships; our public image is burnished, not threatened, by our affiliations; and our sense of control is bolstered, not lost, when we form community. The self, in this view, is *embedded*: It emerges from our commitments.

Identity and the embedded self

In this alternate view of the self, we form our identity not through a series of static personal qualities—sushi, Rolling Stones, Lakers, electrician—but rather through the relationships to which we commit. Other people and institutions don't threaten our identity—they help create it.

Bill Thornton has spent the past fifty years keeping score at sports events for Eckerd College in St. Petersburg, Florida. He's been scorekeeping so long and so honorably that he was inducted into the Eckerd College Athletics Hall of Fame. On campus, he's known as a "walking encyclopedia of everything Eckerd athletics." The Eckerd basketball coach described him this way to the *Tampa Bay Times*: "He's Eckerd through and through." That's the embedded self: your identity emerging through your commitments.

There's even a subfield of sociology, "relational sociology," which holds that it's the relationships we enter into—the social networks we embed ourselves in—that make us who we are. Our relationships, relational sociologists argue, determine how we see ourselves, what we believe, what expectations and demands we submit to, and how we act. In their view, individuals don't have stable individual "substances" that interact with other individuals' stable "substances." Rather, the social world is made up of, as relational sociologist Mustafa Emirbayer explains, "dynamic, unfolding relations."

In the late 2000s, the sociologist Ziad Munson studied antiabortion activists to try to understand what drove them to activism. His hypothesis was that fervent belief led to fervent activism. This is the commonsense view: Someone gets passionate about a cause and then, as a result, joins up with it. But when Munson interviewed the activists in a systematic way, he found that the flow was often the other way around: Many of the interviewees *first* joined an activist group and *later* developed their fervent beliefs. The activists, he explained, would be invited by friends, neighbors, roommates, and family members to an antiabortion event or to join an organization without yet having especially strong feelings about the cause. They would attend or join not because they felt close to the cause but because they felt close to whoever invited them to join. After they joined up with the cause, though, they would start believing more fervently in it.

Stanford sociologist Doug McAdam conducted a similar study of participants in Freedom Summer, one of the campaigns in the civil rights movement, and came upon a similar result. When he compared who participated in Freedom Summer and who dropped out after signing up, he found that the deciding factor in who followed through on the campaign was not ideological fervor. It was how many of a person's close friends were also signed up to participate.

The conclusion: We overestimate the power of our individual beliefs and underestimate the power of our relationships in determining our actions.

The democratic theorist John Dewey tapped into this line of thinking when he argued that it's wrong to think about "the self" and "society" as fully separate entities. The self, in Dewey's view, is constructed in part *by* society. Freedom, to Dewey, was not freedom *from* society, but freedom *through* society: "It is through association that man has acquired his individuality and it is through association that he exercises it." There's a give-and-take between society and the self: You form society and society forms you.

A major way our associations form us is through giving us scoreboards—through telling us what goals are worth pursuing. You only know that you're good at something if others have an expectation for what one should be good at and what it means to be good at it. You only have something to strive for when you have roles, practices, and shared needs defined by a community. There is no LeBron James without society holding up basketball skills as something of value, no Georgia O'Keeffe without the culture of paintings and art museums, no Aretha Franklin without a crowd, and no "greatest of all time" without the ". . . at what?" answered by the public.

When we associate with something bigger than ourselves, we are not only connected to other living people—we are also connected to new ancestry. Christopher Lasch called the past a "political and psychological treasury from which we draw the reserves . . . that we need to cope with the future." Simone Weil wrote that "the treasures stored up from the past and digested, assimilated, and created afresh by us" are the "living sap" we have to create with today. One of the first tasks in forming a new group is to not only gather a community in the present, or outline a vision for a future, but to also claim ancestors—and with them, their "treasuries," their "living sap"—as the group's own. Associating connects you to streams of history that you were not part of before.

When we stop viewing our selves as static and fully independent, we find that commitments—and the communities that come with them—can provide us with a rich, immersive identity. They give us roles, goals to aspire to, rules to live by, visions for the future, and histories to tap into. And it's not just that commitments give us good material with which to fill up our private identity. They also change the nature of identity. When we see ourselves as embedded in our commitments, identity becomes a two-way street—it's not just something we possess but also something that lives in our connections with others. It's not just a source of differentiation but also a source of commonality.

The writer Jeffrey Bilbro calls this *convocation*—the act of becoming and being members in something larger than ourselves. It's all there in the word itself: To be convocated with others is to hear a call *together*, to have a *shared* vocation. Our bonds *convocate* us: make us members of something that expands outward beyond us into others in our community, all while extending into the past to our ancestors and into the future to our descendants. "It is not the story of a life," Wendell Berry writes in one his poems, but "the story of lives knit together, overlapping in succession, rising again from grave to grave."

Reputation and the embedded self

Thinking of the self as embedded and emergent rather than static and independent also changes the way we view our reputation. We fear associating because we're worried our associations will lower others' views of us. At its extreme end, this is what many celebrities do: meticulously curate their associations to maximize their appeal. You can see this in the sports star who doesn't want to take a side on a controversial issue, or the musician who tries to write a song that will resonate with everyone. They try to earn universal acclaim by being abstract and amorphous—by stripping themselves of any alienating particularity.

But in the long run, this strategy usually doesn't end well. We mostly respect the concrete and particular aspects of people, not the abstract and universal. Appearing to others as a Rorschach test might work for a while, but it doesn't have staying power. We have a phrase for people who try to avoid particular affiliations—they "lack substance."

Becoming particular is a form of taking responsibility—for both the good and the bad. It's part of why gentrifiers and cultural appropriators are so offensive: They want the surface-level quirkiness and style of some particular place or community without participating in the struggle that built it. It's also why politicians who join a cause only after it becomes popular are viewed with skepticism. All of this is a form of free riding on the participation of those who were loyal to something particular from the beginning.

Becoming particular is not just about being respected—it's also about whether you resonate at all. It's why country music and hip-hop connect with people all around the world. They're filled with more particularities—particular heroes, particular places, and particular sayings—than any other genre. Feelings get through better when a song is *more* specific, not less. People halfway around the world might not know what West Virginia is, what the Blue Ridge Mountains are, what the Shenandoah River looks like, or what it means to be a "miner's lady"—but somehow connect to John Denver singing about country roads. As the writer Natalie Goldberg once put it, what is more evocative: "a flower" or "a geranium"?

In fact, the best place to find the universal is often in the particular. The Old Testament scholar Walter Brueggemann wrote about how this paradox arises in various religions. He called it "the scandal of the particular"—the idea that God makes his universal plans known through particular people, such as particular prophets who are part of particular communities in particular times. In Christianity, God even becomes incarnate through a particular person (Jesus), born to a particular mother (Mary), in a particular town (Nazareth), in a particular era (during the reign of King Herod). Rabbi Richard Friedman talks about how the story of Genesis moves from grand statements about the universe and then starts narrowing and narrowing. It moves "from the universe to the earth to humankind to specific lands and people" and finally "to a single family"—Adam and Eve and their sons, Cain and Abel.

This is a "scandal," because it seems so ridiculous that an all-powerful, all-knowing being would pick particular people to share a message that is so peculiarly concrete. The reason it happens, according to the theologians, is because we cannot have relationships—we can't fall in love—with abstract universals.

Control and the embedded self

This new view of the self also changes how we view threats to our sense of control. When you are independent and isolated, you have a certain sense of control—you can do what you want, how you want, whenever you want. But when you are in community and united, you have a more powerful sense of control, because you have all the benefits that come from strength in numbers. In giving up some individual control at the outset—by passing through the uncertainty of forming community—you can come out the other end with *more* power than when you started. But to get there, you have to pass through an uncomfortable valley.

The art of bringing people together is about walking people through this valley between personal and communal control. This is what community organizers do: Person by person, step by step, they help groups leave their comfort zone in an unjust but stable status quo to pass through the uncertainty of confrontation to what will hopefully be a more just arrangement. It's what many start-up founders do, too—they tell people to quit their jobs and join an uncertain venture that they hope will, over time—after passing through a few years of chaos—emerge as a stable new entity in the world.

It's also the cycle every married couple passes through. You get married because you love each other and enjoy each other's company. But you also get married because the whole is greater than the sum of its parts—the two of you together are stronger than the two of you apart. To enjoy that shared strength, though, you'll have to pass through the pain and awkwardness of transitioning from the stability of your single life to the stability of your bonded life.

This work is hard. Other people bother, annoy, ask too much of, impose on, misunderstand, disappoint, scare, condescend to, judge, talk the ear off of, hurt, and belittle each other. But there is no community building without chaos. This is the nature of any group of people—be it two or two hundred—trying to find a way to work together. The Jesuit priest James Keenan has a beautiful way of putting this challenge. He says that this is what the call to "mercy" is—a call to be "willing to enter into the chaos of others." Showing mercy, to Father Keenan, is not some grand practice. To be merciful is to respond to all these slights, tensions, and difficulties in relationships with hundreds of little reconciliations. It is the tool one has to ride out the roller coaster of community building. In marriages, for example, Keenan wrote that "the balm of mercy prompts spouses to enter one another's chaos and to forgive each other not once or twice but seventy times seven times."

As time goes on, you find that you need to apply the "balm of mercy" less and less. You discover ways of avoiding conflict through working together and understanding each other. Out of chaos comes community—and, with it, a new sense of control.

The power of community is one of the most well-documented social science findings: When you're in community with other people, you become healthier, wealthier, happier, and more educated. You have more people checking in on you, more people to turn to for advice, and more people to connect you to new opportunities. When the people around you know one another, trust one another, and get along, it is easier to make things happen. But you don't need academic studies to see the power that comes with community—the idea is all around us. It's the spirit behind "United we stand, divided we fall" and "All for one and one for all." It's behind union songs like "Solidarity Forever" and Ben Franklin's Revolutionary War rallying cry, "Join, or Die." It's the idea behind one particularly beloved community-organizing cartoon: In the first panel, one giant fish is eating a bunch of little fish. In the next, the little fish come together to form a much larger fish capable of eating the giant fish. The caption? "Organize!"

But what about that final anxiety of associating with others—the worry that we will be forced to reveal more of ourselves than we thought we wanted to? To overcome this, we need to learn to see this vulnerability of association—Kreider's "mortifying ordeal of being known"—as an opportunity. Community is an opportunity for heroism. What is the hero's journey but the process of showing your community who you are?

Heroism, in fact, is only possible within a particular community's particular mythological system. By this I mean, communities—and the cultures that come with them—are what orient us to what's heroic. For skateboarders, it's pulling off a 900. For teachers, it's getting the most rowdy classroom focused and learning. For comedians, it's sticking the landing and getting big laughs on an edgy joke.

When you feel like you're part of a communal mythology, your daily actions are imbued with the sacred. It's the sanctity of Gabriela Grajeda keeping her Bolivian culture alive or Ryan Gravel weaving himself into the history of Atlanta. Our communities give us an audience to our lives, just as we are an audience to others in our communities. When I am part of a communal practice, the philosopher Alasdair MacIntyre explains, "I am not only accountable, I am one who can always ask others for an account . . . I am part of their story, as they are part of mine."

When the geneticist Susan Wessler first started going to science conferences, she looked up to all the "old-timers." She would be inspired by the "respected elders" who accepted awards and gave keynote talks. As time went by, she saw herself becoming the respected elder to others—and it was an amazing feeling. "You see your students present, and then you see your students' students present," she said wistfully. "It's wonderful."

That's mythology in action: You play a heroic role in a larger story, and it is wonderful. Structure and meaning spring from your commitment, and showing who you are to the world—and perhaps, more important, to yourself—becomes a good thing, instead of something to be afraid of.

Twelve-step programs often take people who have lost touch with their sense of meaning—people whose lives have become chaotic, who feel like they're close to or hitting "rock bottom"—and give them a whole new community and mythology. In it, they find a new heroic journey for themselves.

In middle school, my friend Roger started using. He had always felt socially awkward, and drug culture was the first culture where he felt like he really fit in. But eventually things got out of hand. He cussed out cops, started physically assaulting people, and got arrested for dealing drugs in a school zone. He was in and out of mental hospitals and treatment programs, and got kicked out of high school. Worse, at least for him, was that the trouble he was getting in was pushing his friends away. The whole reason he got into drugs— to belong—was starting to fade away.

One day, a friend from our town told Roger about how 12-step programs were working for him and encouraged Roger to try it out. And when he got to the first meeting, the experience totally shocked him. "I heard a woman be more honest than anyone I'd ever met before," he remembers.

"There were these people there who were just saying they had these fears." He recalls one guy telling him he was so nervous in social situations that before and after the 12-step meeting he used to hide in the bathroom because he wanted to avoid the small talk. "And I was like, *that's how I feel!*" Roger remembers. "It just blew my mind—I couldn't believe there is this place in this world that is like that, where people share these fears that I had built my life around hiding."

But although he was going to meetings, he was still doing drugs and drinking. He could not leave his past life because he was afraid of giving up "that one bit of not-aloneness" that came with doing drugs with other people. But eventually Roger made the jump between the certain (but disastrous) "not-aloneness" of his old life and the uncertain but potentially lifesaving promise of a sobriety community. He committed fully to a 12-step program.

When he joined up, Roger explains, he entered into a cascade of commitments. First he had to commit to the group by attending and testifying to his intention to be sober. He then asked someone to sponsor, and committed to calling him every day. He was encouraged to commit to a practice called a "90 in 90": ninety meetings in ninety days. He even committed to not date for a year while he got clean. And then, of course, he committed to "working the steps." Roger remembers thinking that he wanted to be sober for one year, because it would be the first thing he freely chose and followed through on in a long time. The community gave him the format and the space for him to make and celebrate that commitment.

After Roger worked the steps, he took on a nonnewcomer status in his journey. He started thinking about how he could help others get sober—and started seeing helping others as something that helped him. As I heard him recount this story, I could see how Roger had internalized the mythology of the twelve steps—and how he weaved himself into the myth to find his own heroic journey within it. The more he committed, the more he was celebrated. The more he understood the different symbols, rituals, and turns of phrase that the group used, the more he found belonging. He has a certain reverence for the twelve steps as he talks about them. When I asked him to dissect and rationally analyze a certain step, he said it felt a bit "sacrilegious." You aren't supposed to think about the steps like a lawyer would, he explains. You have to honor the spirit of them.

Roger is sometimes surprised by how much the program has become part of his identity. Recently, he had a coworker who was bugging him. His anger got the best of him, and he blew up at her over something. Then he thought to himself: *What would the people at my 12-step meeting say to me about that?* They would probably say, he reflected, that anger and resentment are poison, and allowing his anger to consume him was like poisoning himself. So a minute after losing his cool, he turned back around, went up to his coworker, and said, "This is not who I want to be. I'm sorry."

Once again, the myth had taken hold of him and guided him back to a shared way of life. "The principles feel alive in me," he said (while adding, in the spirit of the principles, that there is always room to improve). Roger's been sober for over a decade—and he's never felt more socially comfortable, or more filled with purpose.

Association and change

The stories from this chapter have been about getting in line—about conforming to a community's way of life. I can understand why some might assume that commitment involves being some rigid traditionalist. But in practice, it's often the opposite. The community that arises from commitment doesn't just keep us the same—in fact, it's often the best path to change.

Unconditional love—the deep commitment to a full person, rather than to their surface-level qualities—is the type of love that enables, rather than limits, our ability to change. I have a friend from grade school who was known for having a big, goofy personality—for saying and doing outrageous things. As he got older, he wanted to change, but he was worried some of his friends wouldn't like the new him. And true, when he started changing how he related to other people, some of his old friends kept trying to put him back into his old grade-school box. But he had enough friends who knew and loved the deeper him. Through them, he felt secure enough to transform himself.

It's hard to transform ourselves when we're alone. Transformation is difficult and scary—and a committed community helps you get through it. For example, the best way for an immigrant to get used to a new country might be, counterintuitively, to join an affinity organization with fellow immigrants (such as, say, Greek American or Ethiopian American clubs). In practice, those groups do not, as some argue, insulate immigrants from their new country. Instead, they give members the confidence and footing to participate in their broader community. When you have connections that give you a stronger identity, you can dive into something new without fear of being subsumed.

Commitments enable change on a larger level, too. To make change, you need a team that can throw some weight around. It doesn't matter how talented or charismatic you are—most causes require numbers. Liberating people doesn't work without dedicated people. You need tradition to change a tradition, rules to change rules, positive ideas to launch negative critiques, and a deeper morality to challenge shallow morality.

We also usually need to have a stake in a community in order to change it. Otherwise, we won't be taken seriously. Commitment often needs to come before change: Before we are reformers, we must be members. This is why the community organizer Jonathan Smucker is troubled by the word *activist*. Most transformative social movements in history, Smucker writes, succeeded by politicizing, activating, and organizing people who were already embedded in normal community life. The labor movement activated workers in factories, not outsiders. The civil rights movement relied on turning on and turning out members of churches and community groups. The movement against the Vietnam War only succeeded by activating campuses that had already organized young people into dense social networks.

Many people who call themselves activists today separate themselves from ordinary community institutions. They become part of a subculture—in Smucker's words, "a specific identity that centers on a hobby—something akin to being a skier or a theater person or a foodie." Being part of a subculture for support can be useful. But by itself, it is usually not enough to make change. When we're only members of a subculture, we're seen as outsiders and our claims hold less sway. The best action that socially conscious people can take, Smucker argues, is to reembed in the places, communities, and institutions that they hope to reform. Sometimes that's hard, because communities can be unwelcoming and difficult to join. But it's often necessary to change those communities. If you're not saying "we" and just saying "you," Smucker writes, you're not organizing people. "We" is earned through commitment.

This isn't just the case with causes—it's a phenomenon you see in disruptions in all types of areas. Artisans like talking about how you need to master a craft before you can transcend it. Look at Picasso's early paintings—they look pretty traditional. And this is the most true in relationships: You have to earn someone's trust before you can start doling out advice.

In many ways, our whole democracy is an exercise in intertwining commitments and change. Democracy is all about the institutionalization of constant change. It's a system of government that formalizes a process of deposing leaders, changing laws, and keeping a tumultuous conversation open and never-ending reconstruction project whirring. But democracy needs some loyalty for it to work. The political philosopher Danielle Allen writes about how, in a democracy, the gracious loser of a political battle should be thanked for her sacrifice, because she is staying in the game even though she didn't get her way. Short-term winners and losers need to, in Allen's words, "love democracy all the way down" to make the whole crazy project worth the pain of the conflict.

Even at the smallest level of democracy—a simple political conversation with someone with whom you disagree—we need commitment. Both people have to come to the table in good faith. If you're not committed to a deliberative process, it has no chance of transforming you. A conversation you can easily exit is one where there will be none of the reconciliation, transformation, discovery of commonality, or higher synthesis—none of the development of a shared culture—needed to make democracy work.

A dictatorship doesn't require commitment in its citizens'

deliberations—the tension is handled by the powerful. A free-for-all with no shared projects doesn't require it, either, because there's no need to have conversations in the first place. In a democracy, we're working on something together, so the tension that comes with association must be held by everyone. If there's no commitment to holding that tension, there can be no democracy.

Solidarity

On the other side of the fear of association is the gift of solidarity—the sense that, if you commit to something bigger than yourself, then you have something that is committed to you, too. It's the gift of not just becoming a solid person, but becoming part of a solid community, too.

"All men are caught in an inescapable network of mutuality, tied in a single garment of destiny—whatever affects one directly, affects all indirectly," is how Martin Luther King Jr. often described the spirit of solidarity. "I can never be what I ought to be until you are what you ought to be."

Sam Wohns, an organizer in North Carolina, thinks of solidarity as the process of merging self-regarding behavior with other-regarding behavior. We tend to think of self-interest as synonymous with selfishness. But when we enter into solidarity with others, Sam says, our liberation gets wrapped up in theirs. Delaying gratification, not pursuing every single thing we want in the moment, isn't necessarily in our self-interest anymore. And making unselfish choices becomes not a burden but a source of joy and satisfaction.

In this way, our individual pursuit of joy is transformed into something shared. Thomas Merton sees this happening when we *celebrate*—when, in his words, "everybody makes joy" together. "Celebration is not noise. It is not a spinning head. It is not just individual kicks," he wrote. When we celebrate, we are creating "a common identity, a common consciousness."

Maybe this can all be said more simply. When we overcome our fear of association, when we join together in shared pursuits, when we build solidarity and celebrate—we end up with more friends. After college, my friend Alex dove into the card game Magic: The Gathering. While he was in medical school in the Bronx, he looked up stores that hosted tournaments nearby and found a small, hole-in-the-wall comic book shop, the Lair, where people played at tables in the back of the store. Through the shop, Alex found a core group of people to play with. No one else at medical school felt connected to the neighborhood, but Alex soon had a dozen or so friends, from all walks of life, whom he saw regularly. There were grocery store clerks and engineers, middle-aged guys and teens, all races, all different political views—all incongruously brought together by Magic: The Gathering.

What started as Alex's escape from the stress of school soon grew into a community. He'd grown up modern Orthodox Jewish in an ethnic enclave on Long Island. Everyone from his town was devout and communal, and the local culture was organized around tradition and ritual. For Alex, the Lair community bore some striking parallels to his hometown. Some Orthodox Jewish rituals come with a deep obligation to show up, because ten men need to be present for the ritual to happen at all. When he was a kid, Alex remembers people calling his father or grandfather to say: "We need a tenth man." Obviously a card game is different from a religious ritual. But for Alex, there was something comforting and familiar to getting a call about needing an eighth person to run a Magic tournament.

One day a kid named Mark showed up to play at the Lair. He started playing with Alex and the others often, and they soon started inviting Mark over to burgers at the deli after games. Because Mark was so young, the group started paying for him to go to tournaments with them. One day, Mark remembers, he did better than expected at a tournament and everybody congratulated him. He was an extreme introvert, and he remembered feeling like the Lair was pulling him out of his shell.

Mark eventually opened up to the group about his backstory. He had grown up in a rural Texas town. He never knew his dad, and his mom had addiction problems and couldn't take care of him. When he was in high school, to support his siblings, Mark worked a full-time job. He soon dropped out and ended up in the Bronx, where he lived with his abusive grandfather. He remembers Alex telling him, "Mark, if you ever need anything, don't hesitate to ask. I have a couch if you need it."

When Mark's grandfather kicked him out, Mark called Alex—and Alex put Mark up for a couple of months. He helped Mark get in touch with social workers and helpful programs. They eventually found a friendly youth shelter with an educational program that Mark could join. When Mark graduated from the program and received his high school diploma, he invited his dad, grandfather, and Alex to the ceremony, but Alex was the only one who showed up. As a graduation gift, Alex gave Mark three special Magic cards. Mark now sees them as his most prized possessions—and he sees Alex as part of his family.

Mark isn't sure he would be alive if it weren't for the group at the Lair. He's back in Texas now and stays in touch with Alex and the others. One of the other guys from the shop recently traveled down to watch a Spurs game with him. Mark says his time at the Lair gave him the confidence to become a more outgoing person. He feels called to pay it all forward. Now that he's more comfortable, he wants to reach out to the introverted people in his new community.

We know that association can, at first, be uncomfortable. But on the other side of that discomfort is friendship—and perhaps the supreme quality of friends is that they are comforting. If you stick it out through the initial discomfort, the fear of association is eventually outweighed by the comfort of friends. The threats to your identity, reputation, and control become less important than the task of being there for and with your people.

Think about potlucks. Few people actually prefer the literal food they'll eat there to their favorite private dinner. But when we're invited, we still go. We bring our own dish, and others bring theirs, too. If it's an annual potluck, maybe some myths build up—the stories of famous (and infamous) dishes. There's a chance at heroism for the person who brings the legendary cupcakes or wings or potato salad.

It's messy, it's inefficient, and it's not obviously more pleasant than staying at home—but by the end of the night, it's something lovely. At the tables in the chatter about the latest news or the seven-layer dip, community is built, meaning is affirmed, and friendship is deepened. Everybody makes joy.

9

The Fear of Missing Out
and the Joy of Depth

Boredom, distraction, temptation, uncertainty—there will always be threats to sustained commitment. There will always be that feeling, in the middle of a long haul, when we think, *I have one life to live. Why the heck am I stuck at this meeting?* This is the *fear of missing out*, which stems not just from the alternate commitments you *could have made*, but also from all the novel moments you *could have experienced* in your commitment's absence. The alternatives to sticking with your long haul can feel infinite.

Novelty and purpose

The writer Felix Biederman argues that the two forces that keep us going in life are novelty and purpose. We get out of bed in the morning because something new or something purposeful might happen. The divide between novelty and purpose is key to understanding the fear of missing out. Chronic FOMO comes when we over-rely on novelty to propel our lives forward—when, to feel alive, we feel like we have to keep heightening our experiences. When something threatens to tie us down, we're suddenly awake to all the life-giving novelties that commitment might prevent us from experiencing—so we decide to keep our options open instead.

For the philosopher Søren Kierkegaard, this is life in the "aesthetic" mode. At its extreme, you see everything as either interesting or boring. You don't love people—you love falling in love. You go to the protest not because you care about the cause, but because you think something interesting might happen. You don't become part of any place because you love the thrill of being a tourist. This "aesthetic mode of life" is a way to generate an identity without commitments. When no community knows you deeply, your surface-level qualities need to stand out from the crowd.

But even if we keep our options open and manage to find a steady drip of novelty to keep us entertained, we can't keep the game going forever. Novelty has diminishing returns. You can see this with internet fatigue. I remember, in the early days of social media, how much excitement was generated by some shocking or interesting video. You would talk about it for *weeks*. But soon, viral videos only held our attention for a few days. Today, the most interesting thing on the internet has a shelf life of a few minutes. As Theodor Adorno and Max Horkheimer put it: "Amusement congeals into boredom."

Purpose works the opposite way. Novelty is exciting at first and wears off over time, but purpose often starts out boring and grows more exciting as time goes on. When novelty drives our life, we fear missing out on the hot new thing. When purpose drives our life, FOMO is different. We start to realize that if we are always distracted by the hot new thing, the experience we'll miss out on is *depth*. If we don't stop to raise kids, we'll miss out on the chance of seeing them grow and getting to know them; if we don't settle down, we'll miss out on the chance of becoming an elder in a community; if we don't start the project, we'll miss out on knowing whether we could've built something lasting. When you talk to purposeful people—people who have gone deep—they no longer feel the trade-off between the novelty and depth. Depth, they'll tell you, is the ultimate novelty.

Sister Mary Dacey has been a member of the Sisters of Saint Joseph (a Catholic order of religious sisters) for more than fifty years. She doesn't feel like her commitment was a trade-off with keeping her options open. Religious life was evolving when Sister Dacey joined up with her order. Sisters were opening up homelessness services, domestic violence shelters, prison ministries, and refugee aid centers. Sister Dacey started taking up administrative roles and financial planning responsibilities foreclosed for many women in her generation. Through a commitment that might have appeared stultifying to an outsider, she found her voice and was able to avoid the status quo. "My commitment closed off an option to marry, which I would have loved to do," she says. "But commitment grows into options." In Sister Dacey's case, commitment grew into relationships, experiences, and opportunities for leadership she would never have had in its absence.

Grateful Dead drummer Mickey Hart was the first person to use the phrase "YOLO" publicly when, in the early 1990s, he named his Sonoma, California, ranch "the YOLO Ranch." He chose the name because the purchase didn't really make financial sense for him, but he thought, *Hey, you only live once*, and went with it. But the ranch ended up being the way that Hart set down roots. He built a big recording studio in the ranch and convenes people there for different sessions. He hosts friends, new and old. The ranch has become a center for music and community. YOLO, it turns out, was conceived as a message of diving *into* attachment, not freeing yourself from it. *Better go deep, because you only live once.* Hart's ranch turns thirty this year.

To overcome the fear of missing out, we have to make the jump from finding meaning through novelty to finding meaning through purpose.

Depth is a superpower

To feel confident in making the jump, it helps to keep in mind that the power of depth overcomes the immediate pleasure of novelty. Henry Wadsworth Longfellow wrote that we must choose between being an anvil or a hammer. We'll either mold the world, or be molded by it. If you never go deep, you will always be the anvil. And the surest path to being the hammer is depth. When we glide on the surface of everything, we're susceptible to drifting in the wind. We end up chasing shiny thing after shiny thing. And we aren't substantial enough to stop the world from pushing us around. But when we start to go deep, we gain mastery. We stop chasing shiny things and become the "shiny thing" ourselves. When a dedicated person doesn't want to be moved, they won't be; when a dedicated person needs to move the world, they can—they are a person with heft. The depth that comes from sustained purpose is a superpower.

Take craftwork. If you never go deep in a craft, everything's a mystery. Objects just arrive from others, fully formed. The second something breaks, we are dependent on someone else coming to fix it, or are forced to buy something new. But when we go just a few months' deep into a craft, we start feeling a sense of control over more of the world. Six months of guitar practice and you can play guitar for the rest of your life. You take the time one day to learn a new meal, and you can cook it forever. You decide to watch a video tutorial of how to fix your bike when it breaks, and you'll always have a different relationship with it.

If going deep is so great, why don't we do it all the time? Because it's hard. Often, depth doesn't work linearly—it works exponentially. You have to wait a long time, toiling away without results, to get to the inflection point where you can finally reap what you sowed. For example, new artists, radio producer Ira Glass warns, have to survive a "taste gap" to really get started. People get into creative work in part because they have good taste. But at first, what they make is pretty bad. That's uncomfortable, because you know enough to know that what you are making isn't good yet. And you're not going to be able to close the gap until you do a huge amount of work to get better. You have to have the fortitude, Glass explains, to stick it out.

Jad Abumrad, another radio host, relays a similar pattern when it comes to particular pieces of creative work. He calls it "the German Forest." When you set out to tell some complex story, your narrative expands outward. You learn about all these new thoughts and ideas, start having all your own thoughts and ideas, and eventually come to know a sprawling cast of characters. In the middle of the process, you panic, because you are stuck in this inchoate mass of ideas—and are already in so deep that you can't get out. You might feel, Abumrad suggests, like someone who walked into a dense forest with lots of excitement only to lose their way just as night is falling. The only way out is through, and taking time in the darkness to find the way out is part of the process. If you can be patient, Abumrad assures us, you will find your way. And after you have made your way in and out enough times, you start to appreciate the forest as a tool—a "place you have to go to hear the next version of yourself."

Andy Shallal, the DC restaurateur, used the same metaphor in describing what it felt like to launch Busboys and Poets. "When you do come out of the woods," he explained, "there's a sense of accomplishment that is so incredibly energizing that it makes you feel that the journey was worth it." The more difficult the hike, the more fulfilling the adventure—"the more of an adrenaline rush and the more of that excitement that you get at the end." There it is again: the excitement of depth.

The wait between starting a project and watching it come to fruition is painful. Often, it's the process of making a series of promises and then desperately working to make good on them. Take start-ups. You promise investors that you're going to make their risk worthwhile. You promise partners that working with you will be worth their time. You promise employees that their jobs are going to be around in a year. You ask for favors from friends and promise that you'll get them back one day. Every start-up begins with a fantasy story, an unrealized vision at the center of the elevator pitch. It's the depth of the long haul that turns the fantasy into reality.

But when the harvest comes, it's worth the wait. Think about the idea in finance of an "income-generating asset"—something you own that generates income over time, like a bond. By going deep, we build "happiness-generating assets" that pay dividends over the long run, too. You perfected your chocolate chip cookies one summer, and decades later, everyone in the neighborhood still knocks on your door for them. You spend a few months developing a friendship, and now you have a friend for life. You helped get a farmers market going in your town, and ten years later, you're still going every Saturday.

Expertise is another example. It's hard to know what's true anymore. When we make arguments about things beyond our experience, we usually do so based on chains of trust: *I trust this person or that entity who says this and therefore I believe it.* When we first start thinking and talking about something, we're usually worried that someone will figure out that we're just relying on our intuition or our trust in someone else. But when we build up expertise, that trepidation falls away. We know what we're talking about. We can move confidently through some corner of the world. Many people today pine for secret knowledge—a hidden text or proof of a conspiracy that explains everything. But there's secret knowledge all around us: the knowledge of really mastering a cause, a craft, an institution, or a field. The only key you need to unlock it is a little bit of depth—nothing more than your sustained attention.

A deep well of knowledge pays dividends. Listen to someone talking off the cuff on their area of expertise—it's amazing to watch. I used to be the teaching assistant for the philosopher Cornel West, and I was always amazed about how every off-the-cuff line he gives in interviews is so lyrical and illuminating that it sounds like he spent days crafting it. In a way, he did. West's skill didn't come out of nowhere—it is the result of decades of reading every book in his field and building up a storehouse of thoughts, references, and turns of phrase that draw connections between different phenomena.

New York Times reporter Sarah Kliff says she never had the fear of regret or fear of missing out about going into journalism—she loved the craft from the start. The hard part was choosing topics *within* journalism. She eventually committed to health—and has spent the past decade becoming one of the leading health journalists in the country. Along the way, she feels like she got an informal PhD in health policy. Becoming an expert in her field has made Kliff feel confident in her reporting. She can ask tougher questions and avoid withholding judgment in her writing, because she knows how health care really works. This expertise also lets her move fast: During the Obamacare debates of the 2010s, she was able to churn out in-depth, detailed analysis of what certain bills would do on a quick timeline. She can spot promising new stories and figure out what's important and what isn't. Sarah can, for example, read through thousands of hospital bills for one story and know what they mean—what's run-of-the-mill and what's shocking. Don't be afraid to stick to one subject, she advises young people.

Growing up, my friend Alex Prewitt used to read every single issue of *Sports Illustrated* cover to cover. And one day in high school, his mom nudged him to start turning his interest into a craft by asking our local paper, the *Falls Church News-Press*, whether he could cover local sports. The editor assigned him to a couple of restaurant reviews to start. Once he mastered them, he was allowed to start covering our high school games. Fifteen years later, he remembers the first editing advice he received: "Stop being so writer-y."

For Alex, the next ten years were spent honing the craft. He took writing classes, read every piece of sports journalism he could, and churned out story after story for the *News-Press* and eventually his college paper, the *Tufts Daily*. He begged his way onto a night shift internship at *USA Today*, where he wrote captions for photos. He chased down quotes in the visiting locker room at minor league baseball games for the *Boston Globe*. He worked his way up from youth soccer tournaments to velodrome racing to eventually Red Sox coverage. Along the way, he learned the rhythms of sports reporting: writing a morning blog, writing a game story, writing a follow-up blog, and then moving on to the next day. "It's like playing violin or cello," he said. "You work a muscle."

Alex got his big break when his boss at the *Washington Post* called him in to tell him, "You cover hockey now." That Alex knew nothing about hockey didn't matter. "You'll figure it out," his boss told him. He spent the entire summer going deep—watching old games, reading the National Hockey League's five-hundred-page collective bargaining agreement, creating individual folders for information about each player on the Washington Capitals, calling every player's agent, and learning the names of everyone on the Capitals' management and training staff. He remembers when he started feeling like he was finally internalizing the fundamental concepts of hockey—the first time he could identify a neutral-zone trap, the first time he could call "icing" before the ref did. By the end of the summer, when the season started, he felt like he might finally know what he was talking about.

The best Alex ever felt in his reporting career was his 114th hockey game. "I had been around the same people every day," he recalls. "I did not miss a single day of practice or single press availability that entire season. *I knew it cold.*" Alex remembers sitting in the press box, without much prewritten, and cranking out a story in thirty minutes, filing it, and thinking, *Yeah, that was it.* There's something exhilarating, he explains, about "seeing something and then being able to concisely explain what I saw with my fingers on paper."

That's the power of depth, both in craft and in expertise: Once you have it, it just flows.

Alex's story even has a sports-movie ending. A few years after that game, the Washington Capitals made a run for the Stanley Cup. Alex was working at *Sports Illustrated* by then, doing long-form stories. Because of his depth of knowledge about hockey, he was assigned to cover the Caps' run. That year, they went all the way, beating Vegas in five games in the finals. And the boy who loved *Sports Illustrated* had written the *Sports Illustrated* cover story on our city's most important sports story in decades. It sold out all over town. Depth is a superpower.

Atomic commitments

The world needs people to go deep—but we can't all go deep on everything. Farmers choose what to grow. Merchants choose what to sell. Astronauts can't also be zoologists. The first thing an artist does when they begin a new work, Willa Cather wrote, is "lay down the barriers and limitations." Everybody needs a frame.

Narrowing is painful. It can make it hard to commit, because it feels ridiculous to work on a small corner of something when there's so much to do. This challenge is acutely painful in the world of causes. You start working on racial equity in Oregon or air quality in Houston or oversight of the Pentagon budget and you *know* it's going to be a twenty-year struggle. And in the middle of your long haul, you hear there's a human rights emergency in another part of the world or a new campaign finance reform effort or a push to regulate runaway artificial-intelligence technology. But you have to keep chugging away at racial equity in Oregon or air quality in Houston or oversight of the Pentagon budget, all while everyone's attention is elsewhere.

But we should remember that deep commitments have a certain atomic quality to them. Small commitments that are pursued to great depths can explode outward. In fact, the more focused, deep, and alive a commitment is, the more impact it tends to have outside its narrow scope.

Martin Luther King Jr. inspired worldwide movements championing various causes—and he didn't do it by creating a worldwide, multicause organization. In fact, for the first few years of his career, he was focused on one cause (racial justice) in one region (the South). If he was paralyzed by wondering about all the causes he *wasn't* working on, who knows where we'd be today?

The Slow Food movement started in Italy, focused on pasta and McDonald's, and it's still going today in multiple forms. When Jane Addams started a settlement house in Chicago or Dorothy Day started a Catholic Worker center in New York, people started copying the model in other cities. Ralph Nader started his career investigating car safety, but people wanted to replicate his muckraking "public interest" crusades across every other industry.

Many of the long-haul heroes I interviewed made a wider impact by digging into a specific place. Ryan Gravel, from the BeltLine project in Atlanta, now gets calls from people around the country who reach out to ask how they can bring the same kind of project to their cities. A number of Rabbi Schwartzman's students became rabbis themselves. Neighbors of Kimberly Wasserman who were in second grade when she began her coal-plant shutdown crusade grew up to fight for environmental justice themselves.

Art Cullen recently won the Pulitzer Prize for his editorials in the *Storm Lake Times*, an Iowa paper with a circulation of three thousand. Because Cullen stayed focused on understanding and reporting his beat—rural Iowan communities—his editorials have gained national acclaim. No one at the big papers understood the intersection of immigration, meat packing, hogs, and corn like he could, so he became indispensable to the national conversation. If he didn't live by his paper's motto—"If it didn't happen in Buena Vista County, it didn't happen"—every day, he wouldn't have developed the "360 understanding of something" that helped him make his mark.

When you ask people about their heroes, they'll often name people in completely different fields. Barack Obama kept Muhammad Ali's gloves in his private study off the Oval Office. Among the basketball player Kareem Abdul-Jabbar's heroes are the jazz musician Thelonious Monk and the novelist Alexandre Dumas. The TV host Julia Bradbury cites the aviator Amelia Earhart as hers. The inspirational power of deep purpose is boundless.

Many think scaling impact is like inflating a balloon—we make a project wider and wider by spreading its substance thinner and thinner. But scale more often comes by making what we are doing deeper, stronger, and fuller. It's like building a powerful radio transmitter—it's rooted in one place, but if it's robust enough, its message will resonate further.

Combating threats to depth

Threats to depth come in many forms, like the monsters along the wooded trails of medieval tales. There's *boredom*: long hauls get very repetitive. There's *distraction*: the many shiny things along the

161

journey. There's *uncertainty*: doubts about whether you made the right decision or whether you are on the right path. There's *temptation*: the idea that the grass is greener on the other side. Think of all the pictures of other people having fun on Instagram, the flashy new projects launched by others while you were stuck in the middle of your own one, or the flirting from a coworker while you're in a slump in your relationship. There's *mission creep*: the slow change in objectives that you don't notice over the course of a commitment. You create a start-up to do one thing well and some side thing makes more money, so you end up overinvesting in that and wake up five years later wondering how you came to run something you hate. You work on a cause but slowly start fighting for something else without noticing and eventually lose track of why you got into the fight in the first place.

Even if you get past all these monsters, there's simply a lot of *pain* and *exhaustion*. Andy Shallal says people often tell him they want to get into the restaurant business because it looks like so much fun. But they don't think about "plunging toilets at midnight," fixing broken windows, and rushing to work when the electricity goes out.

There are plenty of monsters along any commitment journey, but we also have plenty of weapons in our belts. Perhaps the most powerful one is your story: the one you tell yourself—and even better, others—about *why* you are committed to whatever you've decided to do. This is a story you can return to and renew whenever your commitment is tested. It's why marriages have vows, professions have oaths, organizations have mission statements, and some people get tattoos—these kinds of totems return us to our *why*.

Another tool in our belt is to break our long hauls into incremental steps. Community organizers often talk about the need for little victories. Your first challenge might be getting a meeting together. The next one might be getting representation on a board. Then maybe it's hosting a debate on the cause. By the time the challenge is changing the law, it feels doable.

There's a real estate developer in Dallas, Monte Anderson, who has a funny way of thinking about long projects. "We're going to the moon," he tells his team, "but we're on the bottom of the ocean."

If he worries about "getting out of the ocean and onto the beach and getting in the rocket ship" right from the beginning, he said, he'll "get frustrated and quit." He focuses his team instead on the task that's right in front of them. *Get your scuba gear on and start swimming. When we see the beach, we can worry about getting on the land. Once we're there, we can worry about the rocket ship. There's no use thinking about it all at once.*

Committed people often deal with distraction, temptation, and even exhaustion by limiting complexity. Many of the long-haul heroes I know live very simple lives, because they want to free up space for their commitment. This is partly why many religious figures take vows of poverty. "Fastings, vigils, meditation on the scriptures, self-denial, and the abnegation of all possessions are not perfection," the fifth-century monk John Cassian wrote, "but aids to perfection." Parents, for example, often work to keep the non-parenting parts of their lives very orderly, because otherwise their lives just wouldn't work.

The simplicity that long-haul heroes cultivate is not only material, but emotional. The marriage equality crusader Evan Wolfson talks about how he worked to dull the highs and lows he experienced over his decades-long marriage crusade. "It's not like I never felt the pain or disappointment or fear or frustration," he admits, but he tried to not experience the losses, defeats, and stumbles of his fight as much as others did. He tried not to be as exuberant at the victories, either. He would simply say, "Okay, what's next? Where are we? How do we go forward?" By keeping himself steady, he staved off burnout.

Monte Anderson has a similar spirit in his work. "I have gratitude on days I'm down, just grateful to have shoes and clothes," he said. "On days I'm up, I have to have humility." This attitude keeps him on an even keel. Steadiness has its moments of happiness, sadness, fear, and serenity, but it doesn't bring too much disappointment or surprise, which can be a lot more draining.

The most important simplicity that committed people can cultivate is the simplicity of trusting one's inner voice rather than being pushed around by the opinions of others. In "The Journey," the poet Mary Oliver writes about the experience of finally quieting the voices "shouting their bad advice" and tugging at your ankles. Once we leave the chaotic voices behind, the stars begin "to burn through the sheets of clouds." There is "a new voice" that appears—one that you "recognize as your own." It's a voice that can keep you company on your long haul.

When you make tasks *too* simple, though, you risk boredom. Your story of "why" may not be enough to overcome the tedium of commitment. It helps, some long-haul heroes advise, to notice the changes along the way. Rabbi Schwartzman tells an old story about a rabbi and a cantor hanging out before the High Holidays. The rabbi is studying the same prayer book that has been around for thousands of years. The cantor comes up and says "You've been a rabbi here for twenty-five years, and yet you're studying the same prayer book again. Why?" The rabbi responds, "The prayer book has not changed, but I have."

Even with the help of all these weapons in your belt, you might still need that final *oomph*. For many long-haul heroes, they find it in the beauty of their work. Andi Pettis, the horticulturist, told me that her least favorite task is planting bulbs. "It hurts my wrists, I get calluses, you put them in in the fall and the ground might already be starting to freeze," she said. But in four months, she knows that what she's done will look spectacular. "The display of two thousand bulbs in a planting bed is one of the most gorgeous things you will ever see." Keeping her mind on that scene carries her through the hard work.

But she doesn't just find beauty in the endgame. Pettis says she turns tedious tasks, like weeding, into a meditation. The fickleness of plants humbles her, but she also finds a certain joy in "turning the problems or the tedium into a challenge." Children understand this idea better than we do. Kids, G. K. Chesterton wrote, "want things repeated and unchanged. They always say, 'Do it again'; and the grown-up person does it again until he is nearly dead." They understand that "it may not be automatic necessity that makes all daisies alike; it may be that God makes every daisy separately, but has never got tired of making them." It's no wonder many long-haul heroes have managed to hold onto their childlike awe.

Making the ordinary extraordinary

Our most joyful moments are often the most ordinary ones: dinner with our partner, quiet times with our kids, old friends coming over to have a drink, an afternoon spent honing a craft. These ordinary moments are joyful because they are hallowed by depth. Thrill-seeking gets harder and harder with every subsequent thrill.

But making ordinary life more thrilling through sustained commitment only gets better with time.

Your go-to diner, that old Supremes song, your Halloween tradition, that inside joke—every return has a deeper timbre because it is layered with memories. It's why hearing "Sweet Caroline" played at the eighth inning at Fenway Park feels meaningful even during an average July game—because it's the same "Sweet Caroline" that was played when the Red Sox made their run for the pennant in 2004, the same "Sweet Caroline" you sung along to with your brother at some random game ten years ago.

This same phenomenon can make it hard to tidy up your house. Objects take on meaning—even a spiritual aura—with repeated engagement. The shirt you wore that special day or the couch you had when you first moved to a new city can become hard to throw away because of what depth has done to it. In Marilynne Robinson's *Gilead*, Reverend Ames reflects that "old" can reference not just age but also familiarity. "It sets a thing apart as something regarded with a modest, habitual affection," he wrote. "I say 'old [Reverend] Boughten,' I say 'this shabby old town,' and I mean that they are very near to my heart." That's what depth does—it makes you want to call something "this old friend," "this old theater," "this old racquet."

Depth doesn't just layer specific things with meaning. It also allows us to notice meaning more. Going deep on a topic gives us a lens to see all its nuances. Go to a baseball game with a dedicated fan, and they will tell you that the last pitch was not just a pitch—it was a changeup. And by the way, that pitcher struck out that same batter with that same changeup in the division series three years ago, so it's especially funny. And you thought it was just a pitch.

Alexandra Horowitz wrote about this phenomenon in her

beautiful book *On Looking: A Walker's Guide to the Art of Observation*, where she walked around a block in her neighborhood with different experts who pointed out different things to her that she had never before noticed. At any given moment, we are missing out on the vast majority of what is happening around us. We focus on a few things and miss the hum of lights, the noise of passing cars, the bird on a tree, and more. But when someone is an expert on something—when they have gone deep—they notice more. A geologist showed Horowitz paving stones modeled after those used on Roman roads. A typeface designer pointed out the fonts on the manhole covers. A naturalist spotted spiderwebs and eggs along a hedgerow. A doctor noticed another walker who needed a hip replaced. Depth, Horowitz shows us, makes the world come alive.

The documentarian Ken Burns has a mantra that captures this spirit: "All meaning accrues in duration." This idea imbues every aspect of his work. His historical documentary series are often over ten hours long—they challenge us to extend the time that we'd normally invest in understanding some particular event and, as a result, find more meaning in them. The making of his epics are epics in themselves—his most recent series took ten years to produce. Even his iconic "Ken Burns effect"—in which the camera pans over a single photograph—challenges us to find more meaning in an image by lingering on it a little longer than we usually would.

Ken developed his devotion to depth when he was a student at Hampshire College. His photography teacher Jerome Liebling pushed him to see that "sustained attention" was the key to everything. Liebling taught him commitment to process: the slow work of developing photographs in the dark room, hanging prints with pushpins, and screening rushes from a recent shoot. He also taught him commitment to sustained observation: taking time to see how the light was hitting the top of a building, how a woman's arm was moving, or how two people on the sidewalk were relating to each other. When you sit with people for a long time, Ken explains, the nuances rise to the surface. "In my editing room, I have a neon sign in cursive lowercase that says, 'it's complicated.' Every filmmaker, when you have a great scene, never wants to touch it—and for forty years we've been touching those great scenes when we learn contradictory and complicated information."

This spirit allows Ken to feel comfortable committing to one subject matter (American history) and one format (documentary films) without getting restless. Chuck Jones, the inventor of Bugs Bunny and Road Runner, served as inspiration for this narrow focus. "He was limited to exactly the same number of frames, the same number of minutes for each cartoon," Ken says, "and it was the most liberating thing in the world. It's like a painter—here's your frame, now what are you going to do with it?"

When you're young, Ken says, "you don't believe the actual truth of the world, which is that none of us are getting out of here alive." Once we accept this, we "have to have commitments." Ken flashes back to New York City in 1979, four decades ago, when he was twenty-six years old. He needed to make rent on his fifth-floor walkup—and was offered a job that came with, in his words, "an unheard of amount of money" for a young filmmaker. But he was working on a film about the Brooklyn Bridge, a passion project that he wouldn't be able to continue if he took the gig.

So he turned down the job. "I did not want to put the film cans of the project I was working on up on a shelf on top of a refrigerator and then suddenly, in the snap of a finger, wake up and find myself fifty years old, having not done this thing that I wanted to do, which was to figure out how to make a film about the Brooklyn Bridge," he remembers. So he moved to a much cheaper house in New Hampshire, finished the film, and never left. He still sleeps in the same bedroom, and *Brooklyn Bridge* was nominated for an Oscar.

Even the most boring things can come alive with a little bit of depth. The Baltimore salvager Max Pollock can talk about bricks for hours. When he sees a brick and notices its stamp with the name of its brickmaker, he thinks about the organization that made that brick—a business in an industry in a place, made up of people who went to work every day. All that's left of them is the brick he found, he explains wistfully. To Max, the different bricks in different demolished buildings are a portal to "understanding the industrial history of the last hundred years." He can even read the history of corporate consolidation in the brick piles—newer buildings, for example, have fewer varieties of bricks.

One of Max's favorite moments at his company was with one of his employees who started the job at eighteen not knowing how to use a single tool. He was completely foreign to this new world—and it was foreign to him. Months into working at Brick + Board, Max saw his mentee cutting lumber across the room. When the sawdust started flying, Max saw his face light up as he exclaimed: "Wow, that's some beautiful Douglas fir!" He had learned how to identify the species by smell.

Time

Early in his career, Martin Luther King Jr. preached about the need to have three dimensions in our life: length, breadth, and height.

Length is about our connection to ourselves. Breadth is about our connection to our community. And height is about our connection to the transcendent. If these three dimensions are out of whack, King said, we will be, too.

This advice tracks the three fears of commitment—and the three gifts on the other side of them. When you defeat the fear of regret and find a vocation—a purpose—you find a connection to yourself. When you defeat the fear of association and find solidarity—when you make friends—you find a connection to a greater community. And when you defeat the fear of missing out—through the joy of depth—you find a connection to the transcendent.

Time is our supreme resource. It's made precious by its limitation. At the heart of the question of commitment is this: With so little time, how should we spend it? To infinitely browse is to cut up our time into tiny bits—all out of a fear that we will spend it wrong. To commit is to take a cosmic bet on longer strands of time. That's what the promise of depth is: Though we can't control the length of our time, we can control its depth. And the more time we add to something, the more beautiful it becomes. The deeper we go, the more holiness we find. That's what happens when your depth makes the ordinary extraordinary. By dedicating yourself, you're making it holy.

It turns out that these longer strands of time—and the purpose, friendship, and depth that come with them—are the antidote to our worst fears. In dedication, we find timeless joy. It's not the happiness of feeling good all the time, but the joy of feeling at home in existence. Like Mother Pollard said during the Montgomery bus boycott: "My feets is tired, but my soul is rested."

My mom knits scarves for people. They start out as the simplest of things: balls of yarn. She'd be the first to say that the skills involved in knitting a scarf, once you get the hang of them, aren't hard to learn. So it's not the yarn and it's not the talent that makes receiving a hand-knitted scarf special. It's the time. You take something simple, you give your supreme resource to it, and out comes something lovely. When my mom gives someone a scarf she knitted, she is giving the gift of her time. There is no more holy gift.

III.

SOLID PEOPLE IN A LIQUID WORLD

10

Open Options Economics: Money versus Particular Things

The word *culture* descends from "cultivate"—to prepare some-thing, like soil, for use. A culture *cultivates* us for certain purposes—and a counterculture cultivates us for different (and often opposite) purposes. Young people today were born into a domi-nant culture that nudges us toward, supports us in, and rewards us for keeping our options open. This culture has made the process of dedication—of finding and making voluntary commitments—an uphill battle. At best, it fails to help us make commitments. At worst, it makes us feel weird for even trying.

If you aspire to become a long-haul hero—even if you've con-quered your personal fears of regret, of association, and of missing out; even if you're ready to make a commitment to some particular cause or community, craft or person—be warned: Becoming a solid person today isn't easy. The Culture of Open Options surrounds us, taking different forms in different spheres of life, from our economy to our morality to our education system.

The triumph of money

Until recently, most cultures limited what could be exchanged for money. This kept money—and the markets where it reigned—in its proper place. In civilizations around the world, barriers were set up between certain spheres of life—religion, nature, government, sex, health, childhood, education, journalism, science, and death—and the realm of markets, commerce, and the free exchange of money. The philosopher Michael Sandel puts it simply: Most civilizations have taken seriously the enforcement of "what money can't buy."

The reason for these barriers, Sandel writes, is that certain "moral and civic goods" can be corrupted if you allow them to be bought and sold. The integrity of a democratic election is lost if you can buy or sell votes. The value of honor changes if you can buy or sell public statues. The pursuit of truth is perverted if you can buy or sell research.

Injustice arises, the philosopher Michael Walzer writes, when you can convert power in one sphere (such as money, fame, beauty, or political connections) into power in another. Justice, to Walzer, is "local and particular in character." We set up a local system for how, say, a pastor is justly chosen for a church, how votes are justly tallied for an election, how honor is justly given in a village, how games are justly won in a sports league, and how truth is justly discovered in a research process. When money invades these systems, it has the potential to destroy such local and particular commitments.

Today, many of the walls insulating money and markets have

come down. By the late twentieth century, economists had started talking about markets for everything. They published papers on "the criminality market," "the fertility market," "the dating market," and "the market for votes." Public intellectuals started describing markets as a form of government, where (as *New York Times* columnist Thomas Friedman wrote) "people vote every hour, every day" through their spending. The market was no longer a specific institution within society—it *was* society.

Many of the worries about what happens when we don't keep money and markets contained have come to pass. We can now sell our plasma—and some financial literacy programs even encourage the indebted to do so. We can buy an army of lobbyists for our causes—and buy extra time with political candidates through fundraiser tickets. We can buy sponsored content in the newspaper—or, if we have enough money, even buy the whole newspaper. We can buy natural resources to deplete, mercenary soldiers to deploy, and naming rights to display. Today, there's little money can't buy.

Most significantly, in spite of Walzer's warnings, we've allowed the sphere of money and the sphere of status to merge. Money has transitioned from being just a way to acquire certain goods and services and into a status symbol in and of itself. The rich are profiled in magazines, sung about in songs, watched on TV shows, and asked their opinions about politics and culture. The path to status has become less about local esteem within some particular field and more about how much money you've made.

The old barriers were erected to ensure that money was a means to serve particular human ends. But when money escapes its confines and takes over an entire culture, the logic is flipped: Money *becomes* the end, and particular human goods—like beloved objects, buildings, jobs, talents, crafts, and, most important, people—become the means to serve that end.

Money wages war against beloved particulars in two ways. First, money *liquifies*. When acquiring money becomes the highest goal, we risk seeing all the particular "solids" in our life in terms of their "liquid" (financial) value. They're no longer seen primarily as things worth committing to, but rather as things that can be exchanged for money. You can see this process—"commodification"—in action even at the most personal level. There's that moment when the magic of collecting baseball cards goes away and you start thinking about the monetary value of your collection. Something changes about your relationship to your cards at that point. It's like the light goes out and they are no longer alive. You can see another version of this with family heirlooms. When you start thinking about your grandmother's antique table in terms of how much you can get for it, it ceases to be beloved.

At the level of business, you can see the ratcheting up of money's power to liquify in the rise of "financialization"—the increasing power of financial investors in business decision-making. Businesses have the ability to balance multiple commitments—to their investors, their customers, their employees, their product, and to the communities and places they affect. But in the second half of the twentieth century, the idea of "shareholder primacy" took hold— the belief that a corporation's only commitment should be to its financial investors. This idea began as an obscure academic concept, but eventually became the dominant belief across boardrooms and business schools. Bureaucratic managers, skilled in negotiating between an entity's various commitments, were no longer in the driver's seat of the American economy—financiers were. As a result of this "financialization," businesses started focusing on boosting their stock price at the expense of everything else. Today, companies focus less on long-term research and development, training up a workforce and sticking with them, and investing in the community where they're headquartered. If running your company into the ground or allowing it to be bought out and stripped for parts is best for investors, so be it.

You can see this phenomenon in the creeping commodification of entire communities and public institutions. Where I'm from, housing values have risen dramatically from when I was younger. As a result, people now talk about housing values all the time. Political discussions there are now often framed in terms of whether it will cause housing values to shift. I even once heard a parent argue against a positive change for students because it could lower test scores—and, therefore, housing values.

The German sociologist Georg Simmel describes what happens when the logic of money becomes the "common denominator of all values" in a city. The particularity of everything and everyone— "their individuality, their specific value, and their incomparability"— hollows out. "All things," Simmel wrote, "float with equal specific gravity in the constant moving stream of money." People start mirroring money's "colorlessness and indifference," approaching everything with a "matter-of-fact attitude." The only qualitative question left is "How much?" This is what all these phenomena— individual monetization, firm financialization, and community commodification—have in common: They all involve, for the sake of keeping options open, the melting of all particularities down into money, the least particular thing of all.

When money isn't liquifying particular things, it's *genericizing* them. This is "commoditization": the turning of particular crafts into more generic products to make more money. Sometimes this flattening takes the form of replacing various craft businesses with chains that hawk the lowest common denominator version of products—unique grocers become Walmart, unique coffee shops become Starbucks, and unique hardware stores become Home Depot. Other times, it takes the form of spreading generic practices across an industry. Perhaps the most infamous example is the case of McMansions—the "poorly designed, poorly executed, oversized" houses (to use *McMansion Hell* author Kate Wagner's definition) built by developers on spec, without any input from or care for either the rest of the neighborhood or the families who will live in them.

I have a friend who had a dentist whom she loved. He knew her name and her family, told her stories about his past, and even sent her holiday cards with personal notes. One year, in a crunch, he sold his practice to a private equity firm. After the sale, he was permitted to keep practicing, but he had to follow the new owner's rules. The firm started limiting what supplies he could purchase and what services he could provide. It forced him to use a new software to keep track of his clients. It even made him send his clients surveys to rate his performance on a five-star scale. The changes made my friend uncomfortable. "I'm not going to rate someone I've known for twenty years on a five-star scale!" she said. The dentist soon quit. He couldn't stand being commoditized.

Commoditization leads to homogeneity: that sameness we notice when, on a cross-country road trip, every exit looks and feels the same. When money is the only object, products, businesses, offices, architecture—even landscapes—start looking alike. As the Canadian philosopher G. A. Cohen reminds us, money logic tends "against the truth that people want *particular* valuable things, not just satisfaction of *general*" desires. If everything is "added to or subtracted from the environment in neglect of the value of particularity and variety," then "everything will tend to be the same everywhere," because everywhere has "the same requirements." In other words, if you want "everything to be optimal," then "nothing will be good." I like Chipotle as much as the next guy, but nobody wants *every* restaurant to be Chipotle.

When everything solid is made liquid and everything particular becomes generic, our commitment to the world around us changes. We tend to fall in love with a business when it is both particular (made with love by particular people for particular people) and lasting (existing long enough to give us time to fall in love in the first place). But when everything is bland—made for profit by corporate processes—and easily liquified, it becomes harder to fall in love with the places where we live. And that's just businesses: What happens when the entities that need our attachment even more—our schools, newspapers, houses, and even places of worship—are liquified and flattened by the logic of money?

This dynamic also changes how we relate as coworkers. When a business leader has a financialized mindset aimed at maximizing money in the short term, rather than a managerial mindset aiming at keeping a ship afloat for the long term, she tends to see employees as interchangeable assets rather than particular people. It's no wonder the rise of financialization came alongside an increase in outsourcing, downsizing, and union busting. People are disposable when all that matters is money.

When money rules, employees who are lucky enough to not be liquidated often have their work genericized. Instead of investing in skilled workforces, corporations "de-skill" jobs. Frontline workers are asked to perform rote operations, follow rigid standard operating procedures, and leave their particular personalities at home.

This all might sound inevitable, but it doesn't have to be. Throughout history, various movements have worked to put money back in its place—and, in doing so, imbue other elements of the economy with love for and commitment to the particular. The Arts and Crafts movement in the nineteenth century celebrated handiwork, craftsmanship, and beautiful materials. Its spirit continues today in the rise of farmers and craft markets. The conservation movement worked to cordon off wilderness from the logic of the market. The campaign finance reform movement worked to do the same with the government, taking as its rallying cry "Get money out of politics." Labor unions have worked to force bosses to respect the needs of their particular workers. And this is all without mentioning the many forms of indigenous economics, which often emphasize the particular relationships—to communities and to the natural world—that need to be established and respected in the process of production, exchange, and consumption.

Some walls have withstood money's attacks. We can't sell our particular children, organs, or votes—yet. But the Culture of Open Options is always looming, taking the side of money over the particular, asking repeatedly: Why not?

Too big for commitment

There's another side of the market that is traditionally about commitment: production. Entrepreneurs usually feel committed to the ventures they're building. They own a piece of the economy and stand by it. You can still see a culture of responsibility in many new start-ups—when the organization makes a mistake, the founders tend to write and sign the apology letters themselves. And when workers feel a sense of ownership over the businesses for which they work—as is the case with many small businesses, cooperatives, and unionized workplaces—there's a sense of commitment, too. They stand by the cars they build, the care they provide, and the beer they brew.

But the trend in recent decades has been toward less widespread ownership. There has been a steep decline in unions, meaning fewer workers feel as though they have a stake in their own workplaces. On the entrepreneur side, a wave of corporate concentration, consolidation, and monopolization has cut down the number of founders and proprietors who feel like they own their own piece of the economy.

When twenty thousand acres of land is split into a hundred farms, a hundred farmers feel direct ownership over that land. But when an agribusiness consolidates those acres into one megafarm, one corporation pays one site manager to manage that land. When a coder decides to start her own app, she crafts it in her own way. But when she goes to work for Google, she's slotted into a division inside a huge bureaucracy. A town with fifty retail stores has fifty proprietors invested in the community. But when everyone starts buying their goods online, there goes those fifty community stewards—and, with them, the frames on the walls of local shops showing Little League sponsorships and thank-you letters from the high school band.

This same phenomenon is mirrored in civic life. There is a "production" side of democracy, too: We call it civic participation, or self-government. When people participate in public life, they feel a sense of ownership over their neighborhoods, cities, and even country. You can see it when people come together to build a new public park, reform their school system, or revive the center of town. You can see it in the pride that crusaders in a movement feel when their reforms are enacted, or that campaign volunteers feel when the politicians they helped elect take office.

But over the past century, America has seen a steep decline in these forms and feelings of self-government. In the 1960s and '70s, people started to talk about public life as "the system." Martin Luther King Jr. described it as "gargantuan industry and government, woven into an intricate computerized mechanism." The urban planner Jane Jacobs lamented (and fought back against) the inhumanity of colossal urban "renewal" projects. Robert Kennedy warned that "cities, in their tumbling spread" were obliterating the types of communities "where people can see and know each other, where children can play and adults work together and join in the pleasures and responsibilities of the place where they live." The critic Christopher Lasch wrote that the professionalization and bureaucratization of human care—think sprawling hospital systems, nursing homes, and police forces—erodes our confidence in our own ability to care for one another.

As government and industry became more complex, public participation changed. Much of civic life in the early twentieth century was based in mass membership organizations—religious congregations, unions, fraternal organizations (like Elks, Kiwanis, Rotary, etc.), and political groups (the NAACP, the Sierra Club, etc.). These organizations had local chapters (or congregations or union locals) that hosted in-person meetings, managed an annual calendar of real-world events, and worked to be an integral part of the town where they were based. These chapters would "federate," or band together, into state and national conventions and committees. This structure allowed local ideas to be transferred to national venues and, in turn, efficiently spread back out to local chapters across the country.

But, as political scientist Theda Skocpol has written, American civic life started transforming in the middle of the twentieth century. Mass communication became easier—and civic leaders became enamored with direct-mail fundraising campaigns. As federal politics became more complicated, a class of expert activists who knew the ins and outs of lobbying politicians and mobilizing supporters started growing in Washington. National groups started hiring "donor management" and "member relationship" professionals to get the most dollars, votes, and petition signatures out of ordinary people. Eventually, national leaders started wondering why they were bothering with all the local pageantry in the first place. Soon enough, "membership" no longer meant meeting up in local chapters all across the country. It now meant sending checks to expert activists in Washington in exchange for a bumper sticker, an annual report, and the occasional call to action to send off a form letter to some elected official.

This transition—from membership to management—shifted civic life. Social groups like postcollege fraternities and sororities mostly died off. Groups with an agenda had their local chapters turned into mailing lists. Unions were pacified and demobilized. Religious groups focused more on private piety and less on their role in broader civic life. And political parties that were once-vibrant pillars of local culture became out-of-touch national operations that mobilize from afar.

The consequence of this "civic concentration" is the same as its corporate counterpart: More people feel less ownership over public life. A model where everyone volunteers with, participates in, and lends their ideas to a city's public health system, for example, is one where thousands of people have a relationship with and stake in the success of that system. But when that same health system is managed by an insulated team of experts who only talk with the professional lobbyists from various advocacy nonprofits and corporations, only a dozen or so people take responsibility for its success. You might feel a relationship with your neighborhood if you feel like you co-own it. But if you start to feel like your neighborhood is becoming an administrative unit at the intersection of various indiscriminate flows of action between opaque energy, transportation, housing, and police departments, you won't be in a relationship with it for much longer.

Martin Luther King Jr. described all this as a system that "leaves the person outside": "the sense of participation is lost, the feeling that ordinary individuals influence important decisions vanishes, and we become separated and diminished." The political scientist Donald Kettl describes it as viewing the public sphere as a "vending machine": You put in your votes and tax dollars, and out comes public services. There's no participation, no interconnectivity, no relationship—and no commitment necessary. A vending machine is also an apt metaphor for the type of control that the system sometimes *does* give you: You can't be an owner, but you can be a chooser. You may be separated from the workings of the system by heavy glass, prevented from truly participating in its design, but as consolation, you can choose among options. As Michael Sandel put it, our conception of freedom changed from having a "capacity as citizens to shape the forces that govern our collective density" to having a capacity as individuals to choose what we want among a menu of options offered to us by anonymous and inaccessible bureaucracies.

With this shift in public life came a shift in our practice of commitment. When public life is something we approach as an active participant—as a co-owner—we experience it as a series of committed relationships: to systems, processes, projects, places, and neighbors. When those shared enterprises struggle in the short term, your relationships keep you loyal over the long term—and even transform your original conceptions of your personal interests and ideals. But when we approach public life passively, as an exercise in selecting among options, we never form those relationships at all. There's no sense of loyalty to carry us through those problems. When a system fails to meet or understand our interests and ideals, we feel angry and alienated.

This isn't inevitable. Groups throughout history have fought back against—and developed alternatives to—the alienating scale of modern life. Labor unions and worker cooperatives have fought to build an economy where workers shape their workplaces. Distributists fought for an economy where property is broadly distributed—where community businesses and home ownership are promoted, monopolies are broken up, and crops are cultivated by small farmers. Promoters of the principle of *subsidiarity* flipped the standard "organizational chart" by building entities where the large, distant, and centralized serve the small, local, and human—where the national headquarters serve the chapters, the central command serves the divisions, and the leaders at the top are facilitators for, not managers of, the people on the ground. Advocates for "participatory democracy" have worked to open up government to the voice of the many, believing that we can—in the words of the Port Huron Statement, the 1960s participatory democracy manifesto—"meet with increasing skill the complexities and responsibilities" of modern governance.

Throughout the past century, these alternatives put up a good fight—but they aren't winning yet. Decades after Martin Luther King Jr. lamented the growth of gargantuan entities that "leave the person outside," we still feel alienated by forces that invite us to consume but not produce, choose but not relate, and browse but not commit.

Responsibility and community

In all these fights—between what money can and cannot buy, between the big and the small, between membership and management—the fight is about more than just what type of *system* is more efficient, effective, productive, or fair. It's also about what type of *people* these systems end up cultivating. The stakes of these battles over how we organize ourselves are high, because they are fights over who we are.

Having a sense of ownership over things like our houses, neighborhoods, towns, businesses, professions, government, and country pulls us out of ourselves. In the process, we learn responsibility. Maintaining and improving what's ours takes self-control, planning, and thrift. And when we're forced to make big decisions with partners and peers, we learn teamwork and leadership. The world makes more sense to us because we understand how things are made; how they fit together; and how various processes work. We end up more confident and emboldened—maybe even capable of taking on more than we might have done otherwise.

"Taking responsibility for the state of the world," the permaculture scholar Joline Blais wrote, "is the first step toward empowerment." But none of this happens when we're never asked to take ownership in the world around us—when we're never given a stake in our economic or civic life, and are asked only to be an employee, consumer, and client rather than an owner, producer, and citizen.

It's not just virtue that's cultivated—community is, too. When we keep institutions insulated from market logic, when we have widespread ownership, and when the halls of power seem close to home, we have more opportunities to dedicate ourselves to neighbors, co-workers, patrons, and partners.

The writer Lewis Hyde speaks to this in *The Gift*, his 1983 exploration of the difference between market and gift relationships. Market relationships, he writes, are based on short-term, one-off exchanges. These exchanges can be made between strangers, because they don't require commitment. But gift relationships have a different set of rules. They involve the circulation of goods around long-term communities. They require trust and commitment. To receive a gift leaves you closer, perhaps more obligated, to the gift-giver than you were before. And unlike market transactions, gifts have a synthetic power. When gifts are exchanged between strangers, they tend to establish lasting relationships.

To move between the two modes of exchange is strange, Hyde points out, because they are such different ways of relating to the world. To bill your coworker for using your phone charger or sell something to your mom doesn't feel right, because offices and families operate as gift economies. The opposite is true, too. Becoming friends with the guy you buy a couch from on Craigslist breaks the norms of market exchange. We're supposed to keep market exchanges quick and easy by showing up, making the trade, and getting lost.

One of my neighbors has a contractor friend who helps fix things around her house. Their relationship is a complicated dance. He never accepts payment, so she bakes for him, gives him elaborate Christmas and birthday presents, has him and his wife over for meals, and hires (and overpays) some of his friends for other odd jobs. The whole exchange would be simpler if she just used a handyman app. But that's not the point. Their complex exchanges keeps gifts circulating and deepens their relationship over time. You're not going to get that from an app.

An economic structure can encourage or discourage this way of encountering people. When money and efficiency rule, it is simply easier to encounter everything and everyone as a series of means to our private ends—and harder to find the time and opportunity to enter into dedicated relationships with the people around us. The more we have organized our economy in opposition to commitments to particular things, the more we have lost our ability to relate—to commune. No amount of money can purchase that.

11

Open Options Morality: Indifference versus Honor

In the 1990s, the social scientist Robert Putnam popularized the idea of "social capital"—the benefits that come from having communities that trust one another, share information, cooperate, and enforce norms of reciprocity. "When a group of neighbors informally keep an eye on one another's homes," Putnam offers as an example, "that's social capital in action." When you help a friend move, knowing they're sure to help you when you need to load a couch into a U-Haul—that's social capital in action, too.

It sounds warm and cuddly, but Putnam reminds us that the benefits we receive from community are partially enforced by the hard edge of collective accountability. When people *don't* fear disappointing their communities—if there are no consequences for breaking norms, failing to uphold our share of communal responsibility, or quitting—then communities can't function. Part of what makes us trust one another is knowing others don't want to face the collective judgment of breaking our trust.

"Collective judgment" sounds harsh. But consider 12-step programs, the communities of accountability that help people get sober. Or medical boards that enforce doctors' fidelity to the Hippocratic oath. Or the idea, in union campaigns, that you shouldn't cross the picket line. The phrase "All for one, one for all!" means nothing if, when the chips are down, nobody enforces the motto. Without judgment—not the judgment of prejudice or casting stones, but the judgment of mutual communal accountability—we'd all be worse off.

If a community's norms are healthy and loving, this type of judgment can be a form of care. When someone says, "I didn't see you at practice," part of what they're saying is "I care if you show up." When someone says, "I thought your outburst was out of line," part of what they're saying is, "What you say matters to me." In the short run, you might be irritated. But in the long run, as long as they are expressed out of love and with respect, these kinds of judgments feel much better than being ignored. To discourage this type of loving judgment is to take away one of the key ingredients in the process of making us solid: the thoughts and encouragement—and, yes, the discouragement—of one another.

To be accountable to people is to keep your options a little less open. That's why we're increasingly averse to participating in this type of accountability. More and more people feel they must start every moral claim with: "Of course, everyone can do whatever they want, I'm not telling anyone what to do, but I think it would be good if . . ." And more and more people are worried about being "that person"— the schoolmarm, the stick in the mud—who takes the flak for enforcing norms. It's true that this kind of accountability can be a tool of oppression. But it doesn't have to be—and can often be the opposite. Standing up against bullies, racism, or sexism, for example, is a form of holding people accountable. So is pulling a friend aside to tell him, "If you keep acting like this, your wife is going to leave you—you need to get it together."

But as the barriers between us thicken, getting along smoothly is valued more than holding one another accountable. "Everyone has a right to develop their own form of life, grounded on their own sense of what is really important or of value," the philosopher Charles Taylor wrote of the dominant morality of our time. "People are called upon to be true to themselves and to seek their own self-fulfillment. What this consists of, each must, in the last instance, determine for him- or herself. No one else can or should try to dictate its content."

Every element of this morality is fine on its own—most people today agree that, when it really comes down to it, everyone has to consult their own consciences about what they believe and how they act on those beliefs. But to agree with that principle is not to say "No one should give anyone else their thoughts on what is right and wrong." There's a difference between "No one has the *final* say on your morality" and "No one should say anything to you about morality at all." But in the Culture of Open Options, it's easiest if both are true, because any form of shared morality inhibits maximum optionality.

From morality to neutrality

This tension over whether to participate in judgment, accountability, and morality plays out at the institutional level, too. Institutions— schools, professions, bureaucracies, religions—are often designed to explicitly formalize their own internal moral systems. They have stated values and written norms. They have processes for responding to rules being broken. They have oaths for their members to uphold, storied histories to draw from, and mission statements to advance. Institutions formalize collective accountability.

Yet when we're increasingly averse to making commitments—when everyone must be free to do their own thing—institutions give up on the idea of having a shared moral culture or a shared set of expectations for participants. In place of morality, they substitute neutrality. What this often looks like in practice is a shift in focus from advancing a particular mission to promoting "efficiency." In mission-driven institutions, leaders see their goal as guiding everyone toward serving the institution's mission. This means constantly talking about the mission: celebrating people who advance it, admonishing people who fail to live up to it, training new members in its meaning, and assessing institutional health in terms of it. Often, that means telling participants (at least in a vague sense) what they *should* be doing.

But since we're averse to telling people what they should be doing, many institutions stop talking about serving any *particular* ends. Instead, they swap in talk of helping participants most efficiently use the institution's tools for their own private ends. When I was in law school, I saw this swap in action. The legal system has particular missions: to promote "equal justice" and "the rule of law." But we rarely talked in law school about how we, as lawyers, could advance—or perhaps more significantly, harm—these missions. Yet no one in law school had trouble talking about how brilliant different lawyers or jurists were. In the classroom, it wouldn't be unusual to hear something like: "Say what you want about what she advocates for, she's a genius." The result is an obsession over *means* (one's ability to complete legal tasks efficiently and cleverly) at the expense of discussing *ends* (reflecting together on which legal tasks are worth our time). Being masterful became, as Harvard Law School professor Lani Guinier once put it, "a value itself, detached from what people want to accomplish with their mastery."

This shift haunts other institutions, too. You can see it in an engineering team lauding innovation without discussing what interests those innovations serve. Or a church celebrating increasing its membership twofold without reflecting on whether, in getting bigger, it is still serving its pastoral purpose. Or a politician telling his constituents that he passed dozens of bills last session without getting into what those bills do.

This shift from morality to neutrality often comes paired with a substitution of rules in place of morals. When an institution has a strong moral culture, its mission is made present and alive in the daily life of the institution. Discussions over what we *ought* to do—of what is good and what is bad for the mission—is normal. Participants have a shared storehouse of language, symbols, stories, myths, and traditions to help them better serve the mission. But when discussing what participants *ought* to do starts to seem strange, institutions transition to relying on lists of hard-and-fast rules about what its members absolutely can and cannot do.

The difference between rules and morals is the difference between lawyers asking "Did the lawyer put the clients' money in the wrong account?" and "Is mass incarceration just?" It's the difference between architects asking "Did the firm knowingly send out a blueprint with defective engineering just so they could meet their deadline?" and "Are we designing buildings that are conducive to human flourishing?" It's the difference between a principal asking "Did the teacher secretly change the student's standardized test results?" and "Are these tests helping our students learn?" Rules are necessary, but without morals, certain questions never even get asked.

This widespread substitution of morality for neutrality—of missions for efficiency, of morals for rules—has serious consequences. It changes the nature of institutions from lively and spirited to cold, bare, and mechanical. Moral institutions think of themselves as engaged in the world, asking questions like "How does our newspaper meet today's pressing challenges?" or "What can our profession do to heal this recent divide?" Neutral institutions treat their disengagement as a virtue: "Better not say anything so we don't get ourselves in trouble."

This shift also changes how we engage with society. When we have moral institutions in our daily lives, we learn how to be part of projects bigger than ourselves. We learn how to participate in moral cultures that have expectations for us and that guide us toward missions beyond our own private advancement. We learn how to make change by raising our voice and convincing others using shared language, rather than just disengaging in the hope that something better will come along.

But when neutral institutions fill our daily life, we see institutions only in terms of how they can serve *ourselves*—how they can provide us with the tools, skills, or venues for pursuing our own ends. We relate to institutions as if they were just service providers—and to our fellow participants as if they were just fellow customers. And when we don't feel any sense of shared membership in an institution, it's hard to change it for the better. Being dissatisfied with an institution, we're told, just means that we picked the wrong one.

This becomes a vicious cycle. When we don't engage in moral in-stitutions, we don't learn the habits and skills necessary to participate in them, like how to be bound by a moral culture or how to resolve disputes within a community without quitting. To remain appeal-ing, the institutions respond to our disinterest by thinning out their moral cultures even more—by becoming even more neutral and even less demanding. "No need to make any commitments," they promise. "We are here to help you keep your options open."

From honor to indifference

We can also think of this widening divide—between communal ac-countability and "you do you"—as the difference between *cultures of honor* and *cultures of indifference*.

An honor culture is a culture where honor plays a large role in community life.* In honor cultures, we win respect by upholding community standards, values, and missions. People who best exem-plify them are *honored* by the community. Everyone takes seriously their roles within the community—as a parent, a neighbor, a sibling, a friend, an elder, a teacher, a plumber, or as treasurer of the local Audubon Society—and the community around them takes their role seriously, too. Qualities of character that help in those roles—like honesty, fidelity, courage, and awareness—are noticed and cel-ebrated. Rituals like initiations and inaugurations, weddings and anniversaries, and commencements and retirements exist to mark

---

*This definition is different from some recent definitions of "honor culture," which refer to cultures where there is a greater willingness to resort to violence to defend against insults and other "threats to one's honor."

the passage into and out of roles. When you succeed in an honor culture, your achievements are collective. When one person does better at something, everyone does better. There are opportunities for heroism, because helping the community flourish brings *honor* to yourself and to the community. Your story is woven into a larger story. The more beautiful you make your part, the more beautiful you leave the whole.

By contrast, an indifference culture is one where people don't see themselves as members of any well-defined community. Missions and values are rarely discussed—and celebrations are scarce. When ceremonies are held at all, they are often drained of meaning and can feel like going through the motions. Misbehavior is discussed in terms of violations of rights, security, and procedures. The most we are asked to be is someone who does not get in another's way: a "law-abiding taxpayer," a "doctor who never had any ethical violations," or a "public official who never *technically* broke the law." In place of character and role is personality—identity defined by how we differentiate ourselves, not by how we serve the community. Our accomplishments are personal because there is no larger story into which we are woven. Indifference cultures provide the perfect environment for keeping your options open.

Today, more people are spending more time in communities with cultures of indifference. For many of us, the only honor culture of which we are a member is our family (either the one we're born into or one we choose): a few people with whom we are intimate and to whom we feel accountable. When we spend most of our time in cultures of indifference, we start to experience the world as starkly divided between two spheres: a vast, cold world of indifferent strangers and the warm hearth of our small, intimate group of family and close friends. On a moral level, we start to derive all our honor from how we treat this inner circle while renouncing any responsibility for a wider sphere—an ethic the political scientist Edward C. Banfield calls "amoral familism." And because the outside world provides such little meaning for us, we start to demand much more meaning from our inner circle—often more than any small set of people can really provide.

When our only experience of honor culture is our close family and friends, we never learn how to participate in honor cultures that are less intimate. The sociologist Richard Sennett calls this the "tyranny of intimacy": the feeling that the only way to connect with other people is through the sharing of our most private fears, concerns, and desires. Turn on any season of *The Bachelor* to see this in action. The surest way to woo the lead is through vulnerability, no matter how forced.

But stable communities are most often built in the middle distance between indifference and intimacy—in the realm of neighbors, compatriots, and coworkers. If we feel like those relations are lacking because they're inadequately intimate—or, conversely, if we feel that the only way we can enter into those relations is to submit to intimacy we don't want or aren't ready for—then the communities and institutions based in that middle distance won't flourish.

Ironically, many people are now more comfortable sharing their most intimate secrets with their neighbors than they are entering into basic shared projects with them. Any community organizer will tell you that it's easier to get a new member to give a dramatic speech than it is to get them to consistently show up at weekly meetings. The vulnerability required by honor culture is not the vulnerability of sharing intimacies—it's the vulnerability of submitting to mutual obligations. It's not the vulnerability of sharing parts of your past with others, but—in making and keeping commitments—the vulnerability of sharing parts of your future.

I'm not trying to sound like a curmudgeon. Our culture's general aversion to judgment and skepticism of moralism comes from a good place. Too often a community bent on enforcing its "shared moral culture" is really just one that's enforcing the moral culture of the most powerful segment of the community. In the worst cases, corrupt leaders wield moral judgment cynically (and often hypocritically) to advance their private interests. The essayist Tom Scocca calls this *smarm*—moral righteousness deployed to cover up immoral ends. In a diverse society, we need at least some neutral rules and guardrails. And, of course, tolerance is important—not in the sense of "having no moral culture," but in the sense of having humility about our own *subjective* moral culture.

But there are ways of addressing these challenges without substituting honor for indifference. To acknowledge our fundamental uncertainty, we can, as Roberto Unger has suggested, trade *neutrality*—draining our communities of moral content—for *openness*: preserving moral content while being open to new ideas, divergent experiments, and change. It's the difference between saying "We don't have a shared mission. You do you," and "We have a shared mission, but we are open to discussing alternative ways of thinking about it."

When society as a whole allows for a variety of moral communities to coexist, it leaves room for people to participate in more than one honor culture. This is what the columnist David Brooks calls "commitment pluralism"—having multiple commitments that "balance and moderate one another." When you are devoted to your family and also to your neighborhood and also to your craft, you receive the benefits of participating in moral communities, but mitigate the risks of having one overtake you. Honor cultures, to the commitment pluralist, don't have to be all-encompassing.

To mitigate the harshness of collective judgment, we can trade indifference for forgiveness, as Reinhold Niebuhr has suggested. "Forgiveness, not tolerance," Niebuhr wrote, is "the proper corrective to the egoism and self-righteousness of groups." This idea goes back to the connection between accountability and care. To hold somebody accountable is to see them as part of your shared community. Forgiveness is the second part of that cycle—you affirm someone's role in the community by calling them out, and then you affirm their role in the community again by calling them back in when they've made good. (Too often today we do the opposite—we provide no moral community that might guide us, and when people do slip up, there is little forgiveness.) It's possible to have morality with openness, and judgment with forgiveness—and through them, life-affirming, dignity-respecting cultures of honor.

Mentors and prophets

Think about the people, groups, and moments that have most impacted your life. It's often the coaches who worked you to exhaustion, the teams that relied on you, and the friends who quietly stepped in to guide you after you did something monumentally dumb. For my wife, Lark, it was her summer camp. Her camp in Colorado was a textbook example of a culture of honor. Like many camps, it centered on rituals and roles, values and celebrations, and myths and missions. Each session, for example, began with the campers coming together to create a Code of Living—a set of values to hold one another to during camp. All the campers were expected to work to live up to those values, and counselors could talk to campers about the code to correct misbehavior. At the end of each session, campers would vote on whom they believed most embodied those values that year—and those people would receive a citizenship recognition considered a big honor. For the oldest campers, this recognition was called the Gold Key. But it was more than just an award. For the rest of their years at camp, campers who received it would be expected to uphold their role as "Key women" or "Key men"—exemplars of camp values.

When one of these campers acted out, counselors had the ability to call on their recognition to correct them with special force. Lark's cheeks still burn when she remembers the time it happened to her: when a counselor pulled her aside after a particularly over-the-top lunch hour to tell her, "I expect better of a Key woman." On paper, none of this sounds fun. But Lark—and pretty much everyone else who went to her camp—remembers these kinds of "calls to honor" as some of the most important developments in their life.

It happened to me in my first job out of college. I was working for a group fighting to raise the minimum wage across the country. We were battling giant behemoths, like Walmart, to help raise workers' wages a couple of dollars an hour. Three weeks into the job, my boss—who had a storied legacy of various successful justice crusades—called me into his office and dressed me down. He told me that I wasn't taking the difficulty of the task seriously.

"You're up against the biggest companies in the world and you think you can take them on at the level you are working?" he asked me indignantly. Before I could answer, he continued: "There are a lot of people who went to fancy colleges and think they're smart. And if you want a normal career, you'll be fine. But you're not going to be able to defeat Walmart—you're not going to help raise anyone's wages—with cleverness. You need fire in the belly, which I am not seeing in you."

Never in my life had anyone been so direct with me. And before I could apologize, he kept going: "So, if you want to show me you have fire in the belly, why don't you read five books on Walmart this weekend to get started? That's easy—and that's what's going to be necessary for you to succeed here."

Five books? I had never read one book in a weekend before, let alone five. But I wanted to prove myself. That weekend, I went home and read as much as I could as fast as I could. To my terror, I only got through three-and-a-half books before Monday morning. I came back into the office, full of shame, and apologized to my boss for not surmounting the challenge.

"No problem," he responded, smiling. "But can't you see now what you can do when you have fire in the belly?" Sure, this guy sounds like a real piece of work. But ten years later, the fire he lit inside me still hasn't gone out. In the short run, we want life to be easy. But in the long run, we crave opportunities for honor.

Think, too, about the people and groups who most impacted our collective lives. Who are the people who have left their mark on the world? It's not the indifferent—the ones uncomfortable with speaking of missions, values, or accountability. It's often the people who call us back to our values—the ones shouting, in one form or another, "Dishonor! Shame!"

Take, for example, Benjamin Lay—the Quaker dwarf who traveled around the United States in the early 1700s to campaign against

slavery. Throughout his life, Lay wrote more than two hundred po-
lemical treatises, the most famous of them "All Slave-Keepers That
Keep the Innocent in Bondage, Apostates!" Others pleaded with him
to tone down his moralism, but he refused. "No man or woman, lad
or lass ought to be suffered, to pretend to preach truth in our meetings, while they live in the practice which is all a lie," he would say.
Slave keepers bear "the Mark of the Beast." Lay liked to fill Bibles
with red pokeberry juice so that he could stand in front of crowds
with a sword raised above his head, plunge the sword into the Bible,
and shout, "Thus shall God shed the blood of those persons who
enslave their fellow creatures!"

It's no wonder most white Americans found the abolitionists to
be (as Harriet Beecher Stowe once described how they were often
regarded), "a species of moral monomaniacs." But in the end it was
Benjamin Lay, not the folks who wanted him to be more indifferent,
who ended up on the right side of history.

It's the same with every great crusader—their fiery moralism rubs
many people the wrong way. Mother Jones, the mine worker organizer and crusader against child labor, was denounced on the floor
of the Senate as the "grandmother of all agitators." (It now sounds
like a compliment, but it wasn't meant to be one at the time.) In
the process of securing dozens of consumer protections—from seat
belt and airbag mandates to the Clean Air and Water Acts, from the
Freedom of Information Act to the Whistleblower Protection Act—
Ralph Nader was called a "humorless scold" and a "grating moralist."
When Ida B. Wells started her anti-lynching crusade, the *New York
Times* called her "a slanderous and nasty-minded Mulatress" seeking
"income" rather than "outcome."

There's a word for people like Lay, Jones, Nader, and Wells:

prophet. Prophecy is often discussed today in terms of "predicting the future," but that's not the original meaning of the term. Prophets are better understood as people who call us back to our values and revive the missions at the center of our communities. In communities that become too rigid—ones that go through the motions of ritual absent any meaning—prophets can break through and bring about new practices that are alive with renewed spirit. In communities that have become too diffuse—when, in Daniel Bell's words, "the discordance of voices and the babble of contradictory beliefs become intolerable"—prophets convene people and cohere meanings into a new, living whole.

Think of the Prophet Isaiah. In one breath, he decries his neighbors' hypocritical fasting—"See, on your fast day you carry out your own pursuits, and drive all your laborers. See, you fast only to quarrel and fight and to strike with a wicked fist!"—only to tell them in the next that they could become "rebuilders of the ancient ruins," "restorers of homes," and "repairers of the breach." Prophets disrupt in order to restore. In refusing to be indifferent—in deploying judgment and in calling people back to their roles and responsibilities—prophets are defenders, revivers, and practitioners of cultures of honor.

But when our supreme goal is keeping our options open, we don't want to hear the prophets who call us back to our values, nor the mentors who invite us to become more than our whims. Better to not leave anyone disappointed when we head for the exit.

12

Open Options Education:
Advancement versus Attachment

The mathematician and philosopher Alfred North Whitehead once said that "the essence of education is that it be religious." He didn't mean this in the "organized religion" sense of the term. Religious education, to Whitehead, is education that "inculcates duty and reverence." When education is religious (in this sense), it helps students develop bonds to particular causes and crafts, ideas and institutions, communities and people. Duty and reverence, in other words, are forces that help us attach.

To learn about the world is to take responsibility for it. "Knowledge means responsibility," the theologian Steven Garber writes, "and responsibility means care." Knowledge implicates us: The more we know, the more responsible we are. To specialize in some area is to take responsibility for a corner of the world. The best question to ask throughout our education, Garber argues, is: "Knowing what I know, what will I do?" This urge to respond—this feeling of being implicated—is another sense of what we mean by "our calling." It's another way to understand how we might be "bound" by education—not by fiat, but by a feeling of responsibility (duty); not by rigid rules, but by a relationship with a higher voice (reverence).

Members of the Schoenstatt Movement, a century-old network of religious and educational institutions within the Catholic Church, even expanded this concept to the education of the youngest students. They call it "attachment pedagogy." In their view, the job of an educator is to help students 'attach' to particular persons, places, ideas, and values—to enter into conversations with them, develop relationships with them, and build up an affection for them. Once those attachments are made, the goal is to give students the space, security, and encouragement to deepen them. By doing so, Schoenstatt educators argue, the student sets down "roots of the soul," through which they can experience what it means to love and be loved.

This all seems like a strange way to describe education—and of course, another important part of education is learning how to achieve critical distance from our attachments. But it makes more sense when reflecting on our favorite teachers or mentors. They're often the ones who helped us get into something—who introduced us to Sherlock Holmes books or taught us softball or encouraged us to try out coding or to listen to Nas because they, themselves, were so into this or that thing. Their enthusiasm was infectious. Put simply, our favorite teachers are often the ones who inculcated duty and reverence in us—the ones who are, in the Whiteheadian sense of the term, the most religious.

Institutions of attachment

This approach sees education as the cultivation of attachments. Our level of education is measured not just by the breadth of our options, but also by the depth of our relationships to our passions. In this approach, a quality education is filled with various opportunities, inside and outside of school, for kids to attach to particular things.

These "institutions of attachment" take various forms. A classic example is the idea of apprenticeship—learning a particular craft from a master of it. As *Shop Class as Soulcraft: An Inquiry into the Value of Work* author Matthew B. Crawford writes, apprenticeships help guide us by unlocking knowledge that can't be found in books. Craft knowledge, he explains, is intuitive knowledge. It can only be earned through repeated engagement—and repeated failure. It's like the knowledge you have of your best friend or your hometown—if asked to write it down, you might have a hard time. All you can say is "I just know."

Apprenticeship also unlocks knowledge about ourselves: our talents and limitations, what comes easy and what comes hard. This is partly because craftwork has a truly honest feedback mechanism— the table's either sturdy or it's not, the audience laughs or it doesn't, and the ball either goes in the hoop or it bounces off the rim. You can try to talk your coach's ear off to deny reality—but a good coach will keep redirecting you to what the craft is telling you.

Craftwork provides this honest feedback because it engages us with something objectively real outside of ourselves. To work with something objectively real—something beyond the fickle play of approval and disapproval—makes success in craftwork especially gratifying. You do not have to, as Crawford puts it, "offer chattering interpretations" of yourself to show your success—you can "simply point" at your handiwork. As Drake raps in "Headlines": "When they get my s— and play it, I ain't even gotta say it, they know."

Clubs and teams can operate in the same way. Like apprenticeships, clubs pull us out of ourselves and put us in relationship with something else—a sport, a cause, a craft, or a task. Unlike apprenticeships, they don't just foster a relationship between you and a practice. They also foster relationships between you and other people. Clubs teach us not only the practical skills of cooperation, but also the spiritual skill of being bound with others in a shared identity. We learn how to have our fate be connected to others' fates and our success connected to others' success. Joseph Lee, one of the founders of modern American recreation, thought participation in team sport was "citizenship in its simplest and essential form." When you join a team, Lee says, your ego is lost, for a bit, "in the sense of membership." You share "in a public conscious," and your heart gives way to "a common purpose."

A third institution of attachment is simply the presence of older people in a younger person's community. When elders earn our respect, they become mentors: guides and models for what is worth attaching to and how best to attach. Sometimes mentors show us how to do this explicitly, by telling us to try some particular activity, read some particular book, or ask some particular person they saw in our recent Instagram photo on a date. Other times, they simply model their own attachments and inspire us to emulate them. Elders can create little cultures of honor for us—celebrating our attachments with gifts, making up rituals for demarcating progress, and, perhaps most significant, holding us accountable to our commitments.

When the anthropologists Beatrice and John Whiting looked into how and how often children in various cultures interact with children of different ages, they found that age segregation makes kids less nurturing and less cooperative. When there are no respected elders around to inspire us to commit to something and guide us through the tumults of that commitment, it's hard to get outside ourselves. This doesn't mean that the only way to grow is through rigid deference to some authoritative elder. We learn the most from elders when we see them as a "trusted guide"—when they impel us not through appeals to authority but rather through inspiration and earned respect.

A final institution of attachment worth mentioning is heroes. Albert Einstein was once asked by the New York State Department of Education what schools should prioritize. His reply, perhaps surprisingly, made little mention of physics. Rather, he said that "there should be extensive discussion of personalities who benefited mankind through independence of character and judgment." Einstein thought we needed role models to look up to. This is the idea behind halls of fame, annual awards ceremonies, and portrait-lined hallways. It's why Catholics study the saints and why nations erect statues and put founding figures on currency. Heroes are models of what we ought to be like—and, in hearing about the lives of the recognized, guidance on how we could be more like them.

Heroes help us the same way that elders do: they show us what's worth attaching to. When talking about how they first got into some craft or cause or place, many people cite heroes. Maybe they got into genetics because they wanted to be like Barbara McClintock, or got into prison reform because they wanted to be like Bryan Stevenson, or moved to New York because they wanted to be like Patti Smith.

When a hero resonates, they're like a North Star: captivating us, orienting us, and lighting the way to some new home.

Education for advancement

But duty, reverence, and attachment run counter to the spirit of keeping our options open. To have the type of education just described—to take on crafts and join teams or be moved by mentors and heroes—is to embed in networks of relations and meanings that give us definition and make us less liquid. That's why, in the Culture of Open Options, education focuses less on cultivating attachments and more on training for personal advancement.

Education for advancement devalues craft apprenticeship and other institutions that resemble it—shop class, home economics, music, art, and neighborhood jobs. In place of fostering attachments to particular things, we learn abstract skills and lists of facts. Instead of organically arising in the course of passionate projects, skills and facts are chopped up, rationally organized, and marched through in a sequence. *Unit 13.5: The learner will properly utilize sine vs. cosine. Unit 37.8: The learner will understand the difference between primary and secondary historical sources. Unit 44.2: The learner will correctly categorize similes and metaphors.*

Reverence and duty aren't part of advancement education. The purpose of learning a sequence of skills and facts is not to invite you into a real relationship with something bigger than yourself; it's to give you skills for you, the individual, to use later. When children ask why this or that fact or skill matters, the answer in advancement education is: "It will help your personal advancement at some point."

In advancement education, there's no time to inspire us in

geography class with the epic history of mapmaking, or tell the wild tale of how Pythagoras led a cult that worshipped numbers, or explain the high-stakes battles being waged today over how we talk about history. Better to cut out the fat when there are so many skills and facts to get through. There's no time for unlocking intuitive knowledge, either, despite what's gained in the give-and-take of figuring things out at a deeper level. Education becomes like a train that's chugging along—and if you stop to get a real feel for triangles or World War I or sonnets, you are probably falling behind. Advancement education leaves us with little sense of completion beyond a degree—no culminating work that can give meaning to your tasks along the way, and nothing to point to that really feels like a job well done. Instead we just tackle module after module in an ordered curriculum. The educator Linda Darling-Hammond put the strange nature of education for advancement well: "If we taught babies to talk as most skills are taught in school, they would memorize lists of sounds in a predetermined order and practice them alone in a closet."

Though apprenticeships have dwindled, clubs and teams are still a prominent institution of attachment among American children today. But the ethic of personal advancement is encroaching on them, too. This can take the form of "enrichment" activities— summer camps and after-school activities designed less around entering into community with others and more around personally getting a leg up in school. Another example is the overformalization of clubs and teams—when adults leave children no room to cocreate the experience of an activity with their peers.

At its most pernicious, we start thinking about clubs and teams as individual résumé items that are less about serving a purpose outside ourselves and more about serving our own advancement. There's no harm in a résumé listing what you've done after the fact, but when the forethought of applications and résumé lines looms over our experience of clubs and teams, it changes how we relate to them. You might find yourself, for example, running for club treasurer or vying for team captain not because you actually feel called to do so but because it will look good at some point in the future.

Age segregation means one of the most basic and organic institutions of attachment—learning from elders—is in decline, too. A century ago, it was much more common to live, work, learn, and have fun with people who were older or younger than us. A majority of American seniors lived with their adult children and the vast majority of workplaces were multigenerational. Popular entertainment, from county fairs to community concerts, appealed to all ages—and school was much less organized by birth year. Teens hung out with babies and little kids and older folks, not just other teens.

But over time, more spheres of life began to segregate by age. On one side of the life cycle, retirement homes and communities proliferated—and on the other, child-care centers, preschools, and neighborhoods catering solely to young couples did, too. Work moved outside the home, meaning children had fewer opportunities to see their parents working. (It wasn't all bad, of course—fortunately, child labor laws moved more children from work to schools.) Schools became organized around age-segmented grade levels, meaning kids spent less or no time with students who were four or five years older or younger than them. Entertainment is now tailored to specific age demographics, creating a distinct youth culture disconnected from adult interaction. As Leon Neyfakh wrote in a 2014 essay, "Adolescents, who in a previous era might have spent significant time around adults while farming, apprenticing, or help-ing with the family business, spend their after-school hours on social media, talking mostly to one another."

Today, fewer than two in ten elders live with their adult children. About one in three seniors lives in a community entirely or mostly populated by other seniors. And, as expected given these trends, conversation across generations is becoming rarer. When research-ers recently asked members of the oldest two generations to list all the people with whom they had discussed "important matters" with during the past six months, only 6 percent were nonfamily mem-bers from the youngest two generations. Intergenerational trust has thinned as more older folks view the young as selfish know-nothings and more of the young view their elders as "get off my lawn" cranks. This increased intergenerational segregation and mistrust makes it harder for mentorship relationships to form. It leaves more children with fewer guides to usher them through the wonder and tumult of deepening their relationships with various particular commitments.

Our engagement with heroes has declined, too. A school commu-nity can only tell stories about heroes when the school has a shared moral tradition. To identify figures worth emulating, a community needs at least some shared sense of what members ought to do or be. But like the institutions discussed in the last chapter, more and more schools are choosing the safety of neutrality over the messiness of sorting out communal missions, ideals, values, and virtues. As school rituals thin out, mission statements become less present in day-to-day operations. It becomes stranger to hang portraits, establish halls of fame, and discuss mythic moments. When there is no moral cul-ture, there can be no heroes to embody it.

Education for advancement goes hand in hand with this trend.

Telling us what we ought to do or who we ought to be is antithetical to advancement education. The best way to be honored in an advancement-based school is to advance, no matter how you do it. And building a shared moral culture, populating it with myths and heroes, and infusing it with mystique and allure to compel duty and reverence takes time and effort. An institution focused solely on marching through skills and facts will never provide the space to foster and sustain such cultures.

These two models of education—education for attachment and education for advancement—exist in tension in kids' lives today. On the one side are the informal mentors and apprenticeships, the teachers who carve out time to inculcate reverence for their subjects and the coaches who speak often of duty, and the message that an education is about learning to deepen your relationship with things bigger than ourselves. On the other side are abstract skills and enrichment camps, résumé padding and grade grubbing, and the message that education is about learning to prepare yourself for the next stage. The Culture of Open Options has its hand on one side of the scale: the one that gives us the tools to keep as many doors as possible open, while failing to cultivate the bonds that help us decide which doors are worth walking through.

Careerists and professionals

For those who continue their formal education after high school, the tension ratchets up. On college campuses, opportunities for attachment abound. Students are confronted with dozens of teams and clubs, masters looking for apprentices, new subcultures in new cities, and inspiring professors integrated into their community. More space is given over to cultures of honor—to mottoes carved above doors, storied histories, and esteemed alumni.

But present in parallel is an even stronger message of advancement than before. It's a steady undertow pulling you toward keeping your options open. Clubs pitch themselves as résumé lines and career offices guide you toward whatever will make you the most marketable. Students who take them up on the offer are often accused of chasing prestige and feeding their ego. But in my experience, what ladder climbers are doing has less to do with prestige and ego (or money) and more to do with *fear*—the fear of closing doors. Attaining prestige, they think, is the best way to avoid losing options.

But here's what I witnessed among my peers who let this fear overtake them: The more they tried to keep their options open, the more they became stuck. After acquiring some sought-after job or opportunity, they felt a need to "live up to" the prestige, becoming averse to taking non-prestigious jobs in the future (even when those jobs were what they actually wanted to do!). For some, the process of gaining prestige—of jumping through standardized, institutionalized hoops—made them more anxious about taking a less-standardized, less-institutionalized path. Most simply got used to the world of their first "option-preserving job"—and stuck with it out of inertia.

It makes some sense for middle schoolers and high schoolers to see their task as preparing for the future. It's best not to lock in your vocation when you're twelve. But the closer we get to the inevitable transition from preparing for life to life itself, the stranger it is to never talk about the actual object of the work we'll do. By the time I was in law school, it started getting ridiculous. People were *still* talking about jobs that would help keep their options open. I kept thinking, "Hey, the clock's ticking—when do we actually get to the point? We could get hit by a bus any day now and have never done anything but prepare."

I started to feel like someone had pulled off a sleight of hand. When I was younger, I was told: "This is a means to eventually help with some important end." But as I got older, the message became: "These means—being smart, having a professional job that other people want—are ends in themselves." When people talked about specific jobs or firms or offices, they would mostly talk about the tough criteria for entry. People who were "high up" at this or that firm would come talk to us, but we didn't hear much about the actual work being done—the projects being advanced, the interests being promoted, and the problems being solved. We weren't supposed to think about *what* we should fight for, or *who* we should be. We were supposed to just get wherever we wanted to get—in other words, we were supposed to *advance*.

In his 1944 speech on "The Inner Ring," the writer C. S. Lewis described one such form this contentless striving can take. Inside any community—in "whatever hospital, inn of court, diocese, school, business or college"—you will find "Inner Rings": exclusive internal communities that don't include you. If and when you break into any of the Inner Rings, Lewis explains, you'll find "that within the ring there [is] a Ring yet more inner." He warned against becoming an "inner ringer," the person who—whether "pining and moping outside Rings that you can never enter, or by passing triumphantly further and further in"—organizes her life around breaking into evermore exclusive communities.

Inner ringing, Lewis warns, is dangerous. When we think we're close to breaking into the next Inner Ring, and perceive the reward for entry as pivotal—when "the cup [is] so near your lips"; when "it would be so terrible to see the other man's face . . . turn suddenly cold and contemptuous, to know that you had been tried for the Inner Ring and rejected"—we become willing to bend the rules and sacrifice our values to get in. "And then, if you are drawn in," Lewis cautioned, "next week it will be something a little further from the rules, and next year something further still." The desire to enter the next Inner Ring will never be satiated. To build one's life around it, Lewis warns, is like peeling onions: If you succeed, "there will be nothing left."

Lewis's point is that this inner ringing leads nowhere. But for the modern college striver who has not discovered this yet, it appears to lead somewhere after school: to managerial jobs where the same Culture of Open Options rules. Half a century ago, the standard path to becoming a leader in a major organization was to either create it yourself or to rise through its ranks. The key was your commitment to the enterprise—being a "company man" and bringing "honor to the firm." Most people worked in organizations whose members adhered to what Jane Jacobs once called the "Guardian" ethic, which emphasizes sticking to tradition, showing discipline, treasuring honor, and—above all—being loyal.

Today, it's much more common for the leaders of major organizations who reject loyalty to any particular entity. "Lateral mobility," the critic Michael Lind writes, rules the day: "Diplomats become investment bankers, investment bankers become ambassadors, generals sit on corporate boards, and corporate executives sit on nonprofit boards." The idea of the "company man" has become a relic of the past. Most people understand that everyone advances by jumping from organization to organization. And as a result, most people work in organizations whose members adhere to what Jane Jacobs called the "Commercial" ethic, which emphasizes collaborating easily with strangers, coming to voluntary agreements, welcoming novelty, innovation, and competition, and, above all, being fine with everyone keeping their options open.

For many, this smooths the transition from education to work, because the organizations are designed around the same ethic of personal advancement. You never have to switch gears from preparation and advancement to purpose and attachment, because everyone is still set on keeping their options open. High school is about keeping options open for college, college is about keeping options open for jobs, and now the jobs are about keeping options open for other jobs. It is "preparation for advancement" all the way down. There's a precise word for this: *careerism*. It's valuing our individual journey of achievement over everything else.

This ethic is not inevitable—there are alternative ways of conceiving of the relationship between higher education and real-world work. Instead of designing universities around fostering careerism, you can design them around fostering *professionalism*. On the surface, professionalism seems stuffy. It evokes images of stiffs in suits, "appropriate" talk, and cold, distant interactions. But over the years we've lost an older, deeper, and more inspiring meaning of professionalism: membership in a community of competence. To be a professional is not some individual designation. It means something to *join* a profession. Once we are initiated into a profession, we "profess"—declare publicly—that we intend to perform our craft to the highest standard.

In this deeper sense, professions are not just a set of technical skills; they are, at their best, honor cultures. They have missions to serve the public—to earn and keep the public's trust. They value both technical and moral excellence—and recognize those who demonstrate each. They have codes of conduct and raise a fuss when those codes are violated. They establish a chain of generations, expecting you to first be a student and then to be a teacher.

As Simone Weil has written, professions can keep "alive the memory of all the store of nobility, heroism, probity, generosity, and genius spent" in the exercise of their respective practices. They have myths that inspire and guide their practitioners—and heroes they hold up to emulate. They have rituals, traditions, initiations, and oaths, like the Hippocratic oath. Professions make us think about our success as the profession's success—and, in turn, about the profession's success as our own.

This sense of honest professionalism is what Lewis says awaits us if we quit inner ringing and "conquer the fear of being an outsider." To be a professional "will by no means coincide with the Inner Ring or the Important People or the People in the Know," he wrote. But "if in your working hours you make the work your end, you will presently find yourself all unawares inside the only circle in your profession that really matters. You will be one of the sound craftsmen, and other sound craftsmen will know it."

At their best, professions do not just exist to serve their practitioners—they ask their practitioners to commit to serving the profession's public mission. In exchange, they orient and give meaning to their practitioners' lives. They place you in a larger story. They link you, in Weil's words, to "the dead, the living, and those yet unborn." To be a great Chicago architect is to participate in the epic story of Chicago architecture. To be a great Cajun chef is to participate in the epic story of Cajun cuisine. To be a great nurse is to participate in the epic story of nursing.

In connecting us to these grand stories, professions give us something to strive for beyond our own advancement. In *Notes from Underground*, Fyodor Dostoevsky's Underground Man laments that he "never even managed to become anything: neither wicked nor good, neither a scoundrel nor an honest man, neither a hero nor an insect." A profession helps us avoid this fate by inviting us to become something noble: a professional. If our craft lags, we can strive to advance it. If our profession lags, we can strive to lead it in another direction. Through all this, form is given to our life. We have guidance in what we ought to do.

The philosopher Allan Bloom wrote that "every educational system wants to produce a certain type of human being." Higher education for attachment produces professionals. This form of education sits uneasily in a Culture of Open Options. When one's work is less about personal achievement and more about the deepening of one's relationship with a community of competence, it doesn't exactly help keep your options open.

Higher education for advancement produces a different type of person. At its worst, it produces what the historian and antique dealer Samuel Biagetti calls "IKEA Humans." IKEA furniture comes from various deep ecosystems, but then it's brought to a logging camp, cut into boards, pulverized "in a chemical soup" and pressed "into lighter, cheaper chunks." The composite material is bought by IKEA, cut into components, sorted into boxes, and distributed into stores around the world. At the end of the process is "a sleek but crumbly piece of furniture" made up of dozens of species of wood.

The careerists who are the target consumers of IKEA, Biagetti argues, experience the same process. They may have come from a deep and meaningful community, but they are pulled out of it by their education, drained of distinctive characteristics, and taught the abstract skills, necessary technical information, and affable dispositions to fit in anywhere. They are "modern, movable, and interchangeable."

Biagetti's description is a bit harsh, but he's onto something. The careerists he describes feel unmoored and undefined, but they also have a hard time imagining any other way to be. They may go out in search of a deeper identity and community—of the type, maybe, that their grandparents had. But when asked to make the types of commitments their grandparents made—to really get to know their neighbors, to join a civic group or congregation, or to be bound by a moral community's expectations—they find it hard to take the plunge.

It's no surprise many of us can't. For all the abstract skills we were taught, for all the preparation we were given for our future selves, for all the tools of advancement that filled our private toolkit to the brim—we were not taught the one thing we want most: how to attach. Instead, we were instructed to "never settle." To be educated for attachment is to learn the art of settling—into particular professions, crafts, causes, and communities—and to find there the peace of reverence and duty.

13

The Flood and the Forest

Everything has its time and place—and keeping your options open is no exception. Sometimes you need to cut and run. Sometimes you need the rule to be "I don't bother you, you don't bother me, and we can just go about our day." Sometimes it's nice to learn some skills by yourself, without a master-apprentice relationship or the need to be a good teammate. Money, indifference, advancement—they're all there to help you more easily do your own thing, set your own course, and engage on your own terms.

But it's worth considering what we might miss when the Culture of Open Options dominates everything else. What happens when everything lovable is monetized and commodified, consolidated and bureaucratized? What happens when we no longer talk of missions and heroes, when rituals and traditions lose their meaning, and when no one chastises you when you do something wrong—or celebrates when you do something right? What happens when children are not taught reverence and duty, education leaves no relationships in its wake, and professions are just jobs instead of communities of competence?

Browsing is a nice option to have, but when it becomes the be-all and end-all, what can go wrong? If you look around in the places where the Culture of Open Options rules, you can see the answer: a lot.

Abandonment

Where the Culture of Open Options has taken hold, community participation is abandoned. Private lives have grown and public lives have shrunk. Many people no longer go to civic meetings or get to know their neighbors. More areas of community life and politics have become professionalized—conducted mostly by hired personnel instead of the community as a whole. The public sphere has become a place where private grievances are aired to authorities, instead of one where neighbors come together to solve shared problems and imagine new possibilities. The result, for many, is isolation. We have everything at our fingertips except the one thing we want: other people.

Whole cities have been abandoned thanks to companies keeping their options open. We can see it in the cored-out small cities across the country where corporations have deserted the communities that built them. Residents of Pittsfield, Massachusetts, served General Electric for decades until the company left town, leaving hundreds of jobless residents and a contaminated river behind. In McDowell County, West Virginia, a Walmart came to town, transformed the local economy, and then left after ten years. And we can see it at a larger scale, too: companies that are happy to be part of a nation when it helps them but who pretend they are from nowhere when their nation asks for something in return. Ralph Nader once cheekily asked the hundred largest American companies to say the Pledge of Allegiance at their annual shareholder meetings to remind themselves of their obligations to the public interest of the nation that built them. Only one agreed to do so. Most companies—including many that drape themselves and their products in the flag, talk about their history as an "all-American success story," and ask Americans to bail them out when they are in trouble—responded to Nader with perplexed rejections, confused about why anyone would talk about civic obligations at a business meeting.

The urban design critic James Howard Kunstler travels the country giving talks about how towns have been wrecked when local leaders stop seeing their town's land as part of an integrated whole—a place worthy of love, a "sacred trust" that's "part of a larger social organism"—and begin to see it in terms of how it can serve disconnected individuals and generate tax revenue. He decries the spiritually degrading sprawl that results: "the Potemkin village shopping plazas with their vast parking lagoons, the Lego-block hotel complexes . . . the Orwellian office 'parks' featuring buildings sheathed in the same reflective glass as the sunglasses worn by chain-gang guards . . . the whole destructive, wasteful, toxic, agoraphobia-inducing spectacle that politicians proudly call 'growth.'" Kunstler often caps his speeches by showing pictures of billboard-crowded highway skylines where Taco Bell, Exxon, and Subway signs compete for space, asking the audience: "Is this a place worth fighting for?"

Local community, Jane Jacobs wrote, grows out of chance encounters: "People stopping by the bar for a beer, getting advice from the grocer and giving advice to the newsstand man, comparing opinions with other customers at the bakery and nodding hello to the two boys drinking pop on the stoop." When the bars, groceries, newsstands, bakeries, and stoops are no longer conducive to that purpose—when they have been replaced by forms created by distant entities who have no love for any particular neighborhood—place-based community withers. It's a vicious cycle: Commitments to particular places are abdicated; the places themselves become less conducive to affection; and it becomes harder to make commitments to those places.

Society is held together by a web of trust between the public and the institutions that serve them. But where the Culture of Open Options has taken hold, corruption abounds and this web of trust unravels. Most Americans have come to view our national institutions as closed cartels that serve the few rather than open platforms that empower the many. The more Americans lose faith in our institutions, the more cordoned-off those institutions become—and the more alienated Americans feel from them. This not only leaves us to navigate the confounding forces of modern life alone; it also leaves us susceptible to demagogues who, instead of doing the hard work of reopening these institutions to us, further divide and alienate us.

The legal scholar Jedediah Purdy writes that we can think of our institutions in terms of ecology, the study of how organisms interact with one another in dynamic ecosystems. Just as herons, dragonflies, cypress trees, mushrooms, and otters are all interconnected in a wetland ecosystem, so too are schools, legislatures, newspapers, banks, and faith groups in a civic ecosystem. And just as each element of a natural ecosystem supports the other elements (the bugs pollinate, the trees shade, the mushrooms provide nutrients), each element of a civic ecosystem does the same—the newspapers inform, the banks fund, the schools teach, and the houses of worship gather.

If we do not tend to this common ecosystem, Purdy warns, you have the type of "ecological collapse" that we are seeing in American public life today. As each institution is corrupted and diminished, it corrupts and diminishes the others. Important functions start breaking down. People have trouble gathering, or being informed, or getting a hearing for their grievances. The figures that best exploit the corruption—who profit on the gap between the lingering public trust in an institution and what the institution lets you get away with—start gaining power. The end result is that the ecosystem becomes uninhabitable: People eventually abandon it—public life, a common society—altogether.

Worst of all, the Culture of Open Options takes away our only tool for making things better—the long and steady work of organizing for transformative change. Remember those three pleasures of Infinite Browsing Mode mentioned earlier—flexibility, authenticity, and novelty? They are especially relevant to our political commitments. When we desire flexibility above all, we avoid getting bogged down with any one long-term political cause—we want to jump around from cause to cause instead. When we desire individual authenticity above all, we are afraid of becoming associated with complex, messy, nuanced causes, because they threaten our control over our individual identity. And when we desire novelty above all, we crave more emotional rushes, more victories, and more dramatic moments in our politics. In turn, we are bored by the tedious aspects of chipping away at a cause over time.

On the largest scale, the whole planet is abandoned. When we haven't learned to commit to our own corner of the globe, where the effects of our actions are more direct and visible, how are we going to commit to the planet as a whole? To tackle the climate crisis or the destruction of our natural resources requires limiting our individual options for the sake of our commitment to something larger than ourselves. The Culture of Open Options isn't compatible with that kind of sacrifice.

Identity crisis

In many ways, the Culture of Open Options feels like a flood that has washed everything away. Our commitments form our identities. Once they're gone, we have not only lost them—we have also lost our sense of self. The feeling, for many, is one of being uprooted. Lost is the sense that we live for our neighbors, our comrades, or our ancestors—that we are anchored to some larger story. All that's left is wellness and security: staying alive, seeking experience, and enjoying the ride.

And yet, as Simone Weil wrote, we still have a "need for roots." When we are rooted to something larger than ourselves, we feel "useful and even indispensable." And in exchange for our "real, active and natural participation in the life of a community," we are given sustenance. We enjoy the "spiritual treasures accumulated by the dead," because roots let the dead 'speak' to the living. By participating in a "noble tradition" that is "given public acknowledgment," our pride and confidence is buttressed. Alone we may feel small and weak, but when we're part of a deeper tradition, we don't.

Many people today deeply feel this need for roots. We know that without roots, we're cut off from the past and the future. We know that without roots, we feel more alone, disoriented, and hesitant. We know, as Weil warned, that "a tree whose roots are almost entirely eaten away falls at the first blow." So we start grasping for quick and easy rootedness anywhere we can find it.

One way we do so is through nostalgia. If we cannot cultivate new cultures and practices—or sustain inherited cultures and practices—we grasp hold of the memories of times when our cultures felt more alive. Sometimes, nostalgia is goofy and innocuous—the stuff of on-line memes about nineties television shows and *Time Life* box sets of Frank Sinatra concerts. But other forms of nostalgia are more consequential: politicians who run on reviving some idealized form of the past; community leaders who feel like their role is no longer to steward a living culture, but to ensure their culture never changes.

But nostalgia isn't sustainable. Every time you run the reel again, the picture degrades and the magic fades. The reason we are nostalgic in the first place is because someone at some point created something original or experienced something alive. If you stop creating and experiencing new things, you eventually have nothing to look back on fondly anymore. You can only run on the fumes of an original experience for so long before you run out of feeling and need some new spark of originality.

Worse still, nostalgia is often used to cover up a lack of living commitment in the present. This is why failing politicians try to evoke nostalgia for supposed "golden ages"—it's a great distraction from the less-than-golden present. An excess of nostalgia, it seems, goes hand and hand with present rustiness—and, in turn, those who still participate in living commitments today tend to indulge in nostalgia less.

Real roots embed us in a living commitment that connects us not only to the past, but to the present and the future, as well. Sure, we can inherit treasures from the past that we hope to conserve for the future. But stewarding them involves responding to new circumstances in new ways and bringing our own, original experience and ideas to bear on the commitment. A living commitment is like tending to a fire; nostalgia is like gathering around a fire's dying embers. It might be warm right now, but it won't be for long.

Perhaps the most dangerous trend stemming from our modern identity crisis is the practice of taking a tiny scrap of identity that remains after the flood and having an outsize relationship with it. Instead of it being one part of you, it becomes an idol—and you feel a need to signal your devotion to it in dramatic ways.

Excessive nationalism is a prime example. It's the person who doesn't fight for their country in any real way—who doesn't participate in the give and take of their country's civic life—but drapes everything in the flag to let everyone know that they are a member of their country. On a less serious level, it's excessive fandom. You find some celebrity who speaks to you a bit—and you are so moved by that connection that you make them a huge part of your identity. Casper ter Kuile argues that this is why celebrity scandals evoke such passion. It wrenches our identities when we learn that our idols are not who we thought they were.

This phenomenon—finding tiny scraps of identity to blow up so as to feel a sense of rootedness—has spawned a cottage industry online. It's the reason there's a proliferation of Twitter communities and Reddit boards to help us go deeper into our micro-identities, be they survivalism, vaporwave, Catholic socialism, hooping, YIMBYism, effective altruism, minimalism, or one of the other thousands of subcultures being fostered through social media.

To find these scraps of meaning in our increasingly meaningless culture is like finding a tiny fire in an Arctic desert—you want to curl up next to it all the time. This is why the fights within these subcultures are often so intense. They may be small, but they make up a huge part of the identities of those who are participating.

Most subcultures are at best delightful and at worst harmless. When you mix identity with real commitment and community, your passion is most often harnessed for healthy functions: club meetings, tournaments, celebrations, education, mutual aid, political advocacy. This is the stuff of normal civic life. Most of the time, group leaders—interested in preserving the long-term viability of the culture—try to police extremism within the culture and redirect group energy to productive purposes.

But things get dangerous when you mix the idolization of identity with a lack of commitment to long-term community work. Some people will try to gain status within the subculture in big, quick, and dramatic ways. Many domestic terrorists have been this exact mix: They felt connected to their identity but were disconnected or alienated from any actual community. As George Orwell wrote in his 1940 review of Hitler's *Mein Kampf*, it's the promise of meaning that moved Hitler's followers, not the promise of wealth, power, and comfort: "Whereas socialism, and even capitalism . . . have said to people, 'I offer you a good time,' Hitler has said to them, 'I offer you struggle, danger, and death,' and as a result a whole nation flings itself at his feet." If commitment is the hard and long road to meaning in an increasingly meaningless world, apocalypse is the quick and easy one. And when the on-ramps to the former are few and far between, you will see more people choosing the latter—to everyone's detriment.

This is life after the flood. Many of the ways we made meaning have washed away into liquid modernity. Some pretend the flood never happened, waxing nostalgic for earlier times. Others hold on to the tiny pieces that remain of their former homes. Promising islands of meaning explode on the scene, and then dissolve away as quickly as they came. We are left confused among the chaotic hodgepodge of dueling symbols, meanings, myths, and traditions. No one knows exactly what to do or where to go from here. And all the while, the clock is ticking, because serious crises are festering while we figure out what to do. Our ability to make commitments and stick to them is not just an individual issue—it has immense consequences for everyone. Destruction and indifference, abandonment and corruption, confusion and loneliness—these are the fruits of the Culture of Open Options.

The way out

But if you decide to rebel from this dominant culture, you won't be alone. In dedicating yourself, you are not just rejecting a Culture of Open Options—you are joining up with a vibrant Counterculture of Commitment.

To join with the Counterculture is to enter into a different constellation of heroes, virtues, and meanings, each of which work to invert the values and outcomes of the Culture of Open Options. The Counterculture supports a different type of economy. It values particular things. It rewards falling in love with particular street corners, state parks, dive bars, post offices, clubs, and tiny strips of land with streams running through them. When members of the Counterculture run a business, they care about their particular customers, particular workers, and particular neighborhoods. When they have a disagreement with their community, they choose to raise their voice rather than head for the exit. Most would laugh if you asked whether they're in it for the money.

The Counterculture also supports a different type of morality. Members refuse to be indifferent. They foster and steward honor cultures wherever they go, recognizing the good with celebration and condemning the bad with prophecy. They raise up people worth emulating, yet understand that heroism is both an achievement and a charge—a calling to be bearers of the history and the future of a culture.

The Counterculture also supports a different type of education. For its members, education is about taking on and deepening relationships rather than just acquiring personal skills and talents. When they're students, they prepare not only for the technical challenges to be faced in some future gig, but also for the moral challenges to be faced in some future profession. They aim to not only master their fields but belong to them, too. They know, as the poet Marge Piercy wrote, that "the thing worth doing well done has a shape that satisfies, clean and evident"—that "the pitcher cries for water to carry and a person for work that is real."

An economy that values beloved particular things, a morality that values honor, an education that values attachment—that is what the Counterculture of Commitment fosters. But that doesn't mean that every long-haul hero comes from the same substantial tradition. Unlike Auden's Arcadians and Utopians—who want to bring us back or pitch us forward into some idealized time and place—I am not selling a particular religion, creed, or cause here. The Counterculture's commitments vary—and sometimes, they're at odds. Long-haul heroes might have specific religions, creeds, or causes to sell you. They might think their craft is supreme, or their cause is just, or their God is true. They don't necessarily see themselves as part of a Counterculture of Commitment—they see the culture they are a part of as Islam or Christianity or Georgia or Chicago or Socialism or the Anderson Household or Rugby or Country Music or Ocean-ography. That's the irony of trying to call someone a "committer." When I tried to talk with long-haul heroes about the abstract idea of "commitment," all they wanted to do was talk about the content of their commitments. They are too busy actually enacting their com-mitments to be self-conscious about them.

But at the most fundamental level, this is the question presented here: What do we want the basic structure of our society to look like? Do we want individuals to act like free-floating atoms with a few weak bonds between them—the structure of liquid modernity? Do we want some reactionary or apocalyptic cult to force all the atoms into a rigid line? Or do we want to inspire the world to fos-ter and grow organic bonds—to become a more solid world with more solid people? Those are the fundamental stakes in the clash between the Culture of Open Options and the Counterculture of Commitment.

Tensions resolved

Wholehearted commitments resolve the tensions between the plea-sures and pains of Infinite Browsing Mode. We want flexibility, but not choice paralysis—and commitments help. When we make a commitment, we make one hard choice. But in doing so upfront, later choices become easier. The commitment helps give us maps—principles, goals, or rules of thumb—for navigating future forks in the road. If you commit to going to book club on the first Wednesday of each month, it's easier to decide what to do on the first Wednesday of each month. If you befriend your neighbors in a new city, it's easier to decide whether to live in that same city next year. And if you take seriously your oath of office, it's easier to decide whether to accept a bribe.

Being committed is relaxing, because you don't have to exert as much willpower in daily life. When we have nothing to guide us—when days have no routines and forks in the road come with no maps—we're constantly deciding what we want, what to do, and who we are. Committing saves our energy for more important decisions. And when we're committed, we become less worried about how each of our individual actions will be judged by others. We need only show that our actions flow from our commitments. You don't drink at parties because you're sober. You're going home early from work to pick up your nephew from school. You won't cross the picket line because you're with the union.

We also want to be freed from inauthenticity, but not lost in anomie. Here again, commitments help, for the act of *choosing* to commit to something makes that commitment more authentic. The German word for authenticity, *Eigentlichkeit*, roughly translates to "ownedness" or "being one's own." To feel like a commitment is authentic, it should continually feel like it is yours. In the course of a commitment, you might be asked to do things you do not, in the moment, want to do. But those obligations can still feel authentic if the commitment is alive—if you still feel the connection to that initial spark that convinced you to take it on in the first place.

When you don't want to go to a meeting tonight, but you go anyway because you feel connected to the cause; when you don't want to deal with your friend's issues today, but you do anyway because you love them; when you don't want to follow the community's agreed-upon procedure, but you do it anyway because you think it's important to help keep everyone together—that's authentic commitment in action. There are times when the fire is dimmer or when the organic connection is a little wilted. But when you still feel like the commitment is yours, the relationship holds.

And it's not like commitment requires us to constantly subsume our desires to the commitment's needs. Most long-haul heroes don't feel as though their daily life is defined by sacrifice and self-denial. Why? Because commitments transform our desires. They structure our world, giving us authority to respect, myths in which to see ourselves, and communities in which we have a voice. You learn to love going to the meetings, dealing with your friend's issues, and following your community's procedures because your identity becomes bound up in doing those things. By resolutely committing to taking on those burdens, the burdens become our own. And in becoming our own—in becoming authentic—they feel a little less like burdens at all.

We also want novelty, but not the shallowness that comes with it. Here, too, commitments help, because they facilitate the novelty of depth. Depth provides a sweeter novelty—the type you can only find well into some long haul. What's more novel than finally finishing a marathon, mastering how to bake a perfect croissant, or coming to understand a close friend?

The depth that comes with commitment opens up the world to us—bringing opportunities that never would have arisen if we'd never committed at all. When you're an expert at some field or a master at some craft or trusted in some organization, you enter more interesting rooms. Old friends take you on adventures. And this is all without mentioning the novelty that raising children or being in a partnership brings. Depth is the ultimate novelty.

The Counterculture of Commitment is also the most capable of solving our collective challenges. One of the biggest barriers to tackling the great challenges of our time is the lack of people seriously dedicated to tackling them. We have too many one-off dragon-slayers and not enough long-haul heroes ready to spend ten, twenty, or thirty years reviving places, institutions, communities, crafts, and causes. There aren't enough people who are not just willing to die for something, but are also willing to live for it.

The Counterculture of Commitment cultivates more of these people. They're the people who collectively, through their particular commitments, are committed to our shared world. Public life today is full of chaos, complexity, and uncertainty. But through their slow and steady work, long-haul heroes give form to their corners of existence. They face down the modern mayhem, jumping in and not leaving until they can extract some sense from the nonsense. Then they go one step further: They turn understanding into action, and ideas into projects. To find insight in a piece of the present—and then, with it, to forge a piece of the future—seems miraculous. But with a bit of sustained effort—which stems from a bit of commitment—it's possible. The dedicated do it all the time.

Democracy requires, to use a Thomas Carlyle phrase, "a whole world of heroes." One of the best arguments for democracy is that the world is too much for a small class of leaders to handle. In the face of uncertainty and complexity, a nation can set about on millions of distributed experiments. When many people are committed and empowered enough to respond to various challenges at various levels, you don't need a blueprint to manage the world. The people themselves become a robust organism capable of responding to the different needs and challenges we face. But for this to work, we all have to play our part—and that requires making commitments.

For some, it may seem like a letdown to think of the great work of public life as the making and honoring of commitments. But here's the thing about dedication: By saying you are willing to work at something for a long time, you free your imagination. If we only focus on those projects that we can get done quickly, what we believe to be possible is limited. But if we're willing to go slow, we can embrace grander visions, knowing that we have the time and patience to make them real. It's no coincidence that the most transformative figures in history were also the most dedicated.

Reforestation

Earlier, I told a story about a flood. Organic communities grew up in various places over time. In the modern age, many of them were uprooted and rationalized—what Bauman called "solid modernity." And in recent decades, we've watched as the old organic communities continued to be uprooted, only for the modern structures that replaced them to be beset by deconstruction, disruption, and corruption. Many of us feel bereft. We are disconnected from the old communities of myth, tradition, and ritual, and from the new structures that were supposed to be their fair and trustworthy replacements. We are left grasping onto tiny shreds of meaning and worshipping them in an outsized fashion, or giving up on finding any meaning at all and settling for surfing the waves of liquid modernity.

The Counterculture responds to the flood by starting to cultivate again. They plant and foster new relationships. And slowly, over time, commitment by commitment, seed by seed, they lay down new roots. The Counterculture of Commitment is a reforestation project.

In his 1953 short story, "The Man Who Planted Trees," Jean Giono writes of a small French village where the air was dry, the wind was biting, the grass was coarse, and the neighbors were full of rivalry. One man, Elzéard Bouffier, couldn't take it anymore. So one day, he went out into the arid land with an iron rod and started making a line of holes in the ground. In each hole, he placed acorns, one by one. Over the course of three years, he repeated the task daily, eventually planting one hundred thousand acorns. Twenty thousand sprouted. Bouffier tended to them each day, "determinedly pursuing his task in all its simplicity."

Eventually, ten thousand oaks grew up, taller than people. And suddenly, "creation seemed to come about in a sort of chain reaction." Water started flowing in the brooks that had once been dry. The wind scattered seeds, and trees started appearing in surprising places. "There reappeared willows, rushes, meadows, gardens, flowers, and a certain purpose in being alive," Giono writes. The roads in the nearby villages were soon filled with "hearty men and women, boys and girls who understand laughter and have recovered a taste for picnics." The transformation was so gradual that nobody was astonished on any particular day. What happened was only remarkable in retrospect. It was all because "one man, armed only with his own physical and moral resources, was able to cause this land of Canaan to spring from the wasteland."

Father Józef Tischner, the first chaplain of the Solidarity movement in Poland, told a similar story of how change happens. He compares the spread of conscientiousness to the planting of trees. "Someone plants a tree—one, a second, a third, many trees," he wrote, and "from those trees grows a forest." Once the forest is there, it can't be ignored; it is like "the earth under our feet." Change doesn't always mean a grand battle, Tischner argued. Often, the forest just grows into existence and "the reality of the forest cannot be disregarded" by the powers that be. A forest fights its enemies, Tischner argued, by "growing and becoming an even larger forest," just as "solidarity of conscience fights its opponents by becoming more of a conscience and more of a solidarity."

What holds the forest together? In Tischner's view, it is *fidelity*—everyone's commitments to their relationships with each other. When members of a movement say they're hopeful about the future, they're saying that they trust everybody else in the movement to remain committed like they are. "The source of my hope, its power and light," Tischner wrote, "is the person entrusted with my hope." To say "I trust you" is to say "in you I put my hope."

The Counterculture of Commitment is made up of people who are tilling the soil, planting seeds, and growing small forests—and, in doing so, they are generating hope. Their commitments don't just transform society—they transform the committers themselves. In doing this work, these sowers are demonstrating a way out of our identity crisis.

Some say our uprootedness is permanent, that when our connection to our ancestors washed away in the flood, there's nothing left to root us. But what these pessimists fail to recognize is that our roots are not only to be found in the past. We are rooted not just by our ancestors, but by our descendants, as well. Our roots can lie in the future. When we make a commitment, we become closer to the future, and closer to our descendants whom our commitments serve. We summon our descendants—the people who will benefit from the fruits of our work—by dedicating ourselves to things. If we can no longer live for the past, because it has been washed away, we can live for the future—and in doing so, be rooted to it.

Earlier I mentioned that *dedicate* has two meanings—to make something holy and to stick at something for a long time. We do something holy in those few extraordinary moments when we make commitments. And we do something holy in those countless ordinary moments when we keep them.

In the most dedicated people I have known, I have witnessed how that pursuit of holiness comes with a side effect of immense joy. You can see that joy in the eyes of dedicated older people, who experience so deeply what the poet Jack Gilbert once called "the beauty that is of many days, steady and clear . . . the normal excellence of long accomplishment."

14

An Invitation

"Yes! Can I Help?"

In 1985, Karen Washington, a physical therapist and single mother of two, moved from Harlem to the Bronx. She had never owned a home, and her new brick row house made her feel like she finally had part of the American dream.

There was only one problem: Across the street from Karen's new home was a vacant lot that was filled with garbage. She and her neighbors had been assured that another row house would be built there, but months turned into years and construction crews never showed up. "My American dream became my American nightmare," she remembers. She wondered why she even moved to the Bronx if it meant she was just going to spend every day staring out her kitchen window at a pile of trash. "For me," she remembered about the time, "it was a lot of despair, hopelessness, and anger."

But one day in 1988, Karen looked out her window and saw something new across the street. One of her neighbors, Jose Lugo, was standing in the vacant lot with a shovel. "My eyes lit up like a Christmas tree," she remembers. She walked across the street and asked Jose what was going on. He told her he was thinking of clearing out the trash and planting a community garden. "Yes!" Karen exclaimed. "Can I help?"

Karen and Jose set to work gathering people in the community to join the effort. Day by day, they helped clear the trash. Eventually, they started planting. Karen had no idea how to garden at first. All she knew was you had to put seeds in the ground and water them. So that's what she did. She and her neighbors would soon fill the plots with corn and squash, kale and collard greens, cantaloupe and string beans, hens and holly bushes, and more. The effort was such a success that, within a year, the neighborhood was able to petition the city to declare the vacant lot an official community garden. A sign went up out front: "The Garden of Happiness."

The more time Karen spent in the garden, the more she got to know her neighbors. And as she did, she started to learn about how other public problems affected them. "I was hearing and feeling the social issues that were happening around me," she recalls. "I'm in the garden and I hear people say, 'We have no heat, we don't have hot water,' or 'We can't afford a place to live,' or 'My children are going to school, and they have forty kids in the classroom.'"

So Karen got involved in causes beyond the Garden of Happiness. She joined together with other community gardeners to form La Familia Verde, a coalition to advocate, educate, and create at a larger scale in the city. She started sitting on the boards of food justice and hunger alleviation organizations. She cofounded Black

Urban Growers to raise up the voices of Black farmers and gardeners in the food justice movement.

Along the way, Karen honed her craft. She picked up tips and tricks from Jose and other community gardeners. She started apprenticing at a farm in upstate New York. She even went to California to take courses on organic farming with people decades younger than her. The Bronx physical therapist who once knew nothing beyond putting seeds in the ground and watering them now co-owns an organic farm upstate, Rise & Root Farm. She is now known around the country as the Queen of Urban Growing. And the Garden of Happiness? Three decades after Karen decided to walk over to Jose and say "Yes! Can I help?," it's still going strong, bringing joy and community to the neighbors of Prospect Avenue—some of whom weren't even born when Karen started planting seeds.

Gardening

Anne Lamott has called the garden one of "the two great metaphors for humanity." ("The other, of course, is the river.") Gardening is certainly the great metaphor for commitment. When we plant a garden, we dedicate ourselves to doing a lot of work without immediate gratification—all with hope in some beautiful bounty that may (or may not) emerge at some point in the future. Gardening is not quick and mechanical—it's slow and organic. Gardens are delicate at first, but they can grow into robust ecosystems. Tending to them resembles a relationship—you have some power over what you plant, but your plants also have their own plans. "You can't grab a tomato plant by the stem and demand it produce tomatoes," the writer Mark T. Mitchell says. You also can't grow everything everywhere, because particularity matters. Mitchell puts it bluntly: "You can't grow bananas in Wyoming."

Gardening, like commitment, requires a certain level of rootedness. You have to tend to plants consistently—you can't chaotically bop in and out of gardening. And if you need to take a break from your plants, the only way to do so without killing them is to build community—to invite others to join you in your garden.

The writer Janna Malamud Smith argues that "the good life is lived best" by those with a garden or "the moral equivalent of a garden": "Life is better when you possess a sustaining practice that holds your desire, demands your attention, and requires effort; a plot of ground that gratifies the wish to labor and create." This is a "generative, hardy way to live in the world . . . and your reward is that in some seasons you create a gratifying bounty."

That "gratifying bounty" is the final connection between gardening and dedication: Both are sources of great joy. Karen Washington told me that she thanks God every day for how great her life is. Gardening—both literal and figurative—takes time, she insists. But in the hard times, you have to look at the big picture and have faith. "I knew regardless that something was going to happen with that empty lot," she says. "I knew with my heart and soul that we were not going to be there the rest of our lives looking at that empty lot."

"Every day, I get up and I'm saying good morning to people," Karen told me. "I look at the trees and I'm thankful for the trees, I'm thankful for the sky, I'm just thankful for life!" When she's on a crowded elevator, and everyone's looking at the floor and no one's saying anything, Karen tries to say something to make a difference in those people's days. "For me, every day is Thanksgiving, every day is Christmas. It's not a certain day to celebrate life—it's each and every day." Turns out that the Garden of Happiness isn't just on Prospect Avenue—it's everywhere Karen goes.

The vacant lots of life

Many of us find ourselves in a similar situation to the one Karen found herself in. We arrive in life and discover various vacant lots right outside our front doors. No one seems to be in charge of them—the powers that be are nowhere to be found. And the longer the lots sit vacant, the worse they get.

When faced with the vacant lots of life, some choose to do nothing. The excuses pile up with the trash: "I have no experience with this"; "I bet someone else is in charge of this"; "I'll just focus on what's going on inside my house, not across the street." For some, this passivity curdles into endless chatter—constant talk about how somebody should do something about the vacant lots. Others choose to move—to hit the road in the hopes of finding some clean paradise, leaving those left behind to deal with the garbage pile.

Take it or leave it: these seem to be the options most people are choosing from these days. But Karen Washington and people like her are living out a third option: dedicating themselves to turning the vacant lots of life into something different. They are entering into relationships with them and sticking with those relationships until something living emerges. They are responding to an invitation to commit with a hearty "Yes! Can I help?"—and following through over the long haul. They are not *taking* it or *leaving* it, but *transforming* it.

When we commit, we aren't doing something small. Our dedication is not like a drop in the ocean. It's like a fire in the darkness that could become a blaze, or a stream carving out a path that could become a canyon, or a seed planted in the cracks of the concrete that could become an oak. It is life! And life is generative—it grows, spreads, reproduces, and, most important, supports other life.

This is what Dorothy Day meant when she said we fight futility when we make peace with laying "one brick at a time," taking "one step at a time," and begging "for an increase of love in our hearts that will vitalize and transform these actions." It's why the Reverend William L. Watkinson preached that it is "far better to light the candle than to curse the darkness." It's why Wendell Berry thought that "in the dark of the moon, in flying snow, in the dead of winter, war spreading, families dying, the world in danger," the best thing to do was to "walk the rocky hillside, sowing clover." A piece of life in a deadened world is not a tiny thing—it is everything. And if by our commitments we bring to life a few once-vacant lots that can stand in contrast to the bleak world around them, those small alternatives are already triumphant—a vibrant future already alive in the present.

There are people all around the world who have made the choice Karen did—to respond to an invitation to dedicate themselves to transforming some vacant lot of life into a lush garden. Place by place, cause by cause, craft by craft, person by person, they are revitalizing the world.

It's our turn to respond to this invitation, too.

So what are we waiting for? Come grab a trowel.

INFLUENCES

My journey into understanding Infinite Browsing Mode, the Counterculture of Commitment, and the meaning of dedication was aided by countless dedicated thinkers. If you are interested in reading further on this topic, here are some of those influences.

The greatest influence on this book is *Liquid Modernity*, a masterful work by the Polish sociologist Zygmunt Bauman. Bauman's writing is full of deep and simple images that elucidate complex concepts in modern society.

The best work on the direct psychological experience of being stuck in Infinite Browsing Mode is Barry Schwartz's *The Paradox of Choice*, which explains why having more options only makes us happier up until a point, after which choice begins to tyrannize us. Schwartz has a gift for illuminating how our individual psychology interacts with our broader social structure.

The work of two grand thinkers from the same late-nineteenth-century generation—Émile Durkheim and William James—were helpful in explaining the listlessness that stems from lack of purposeful commitment and community. James and his fellow Pragmatists, such as John Dewey, greatly informed my thoughts on how we must sometimes jump into a commitment before we fully know that it is right.

Lingering in the background of many of my arguments is a story about intellectual and cultural history: how constellations of meaning have been broken up and repeatedly rearranged in the meat grinder of deconstruction, forcing individuals to navigate alone through the chaos as the curator of their own private mythology. In building my understanding of this history, the writings of Romano Guardini, Charles Taylor, and Alasdair MacIntyre on the meaning of modern secularism and individualism were helpful, as were Daniel T. Rodgers's *Age of Fracture* and Daniel Bell's *The Cultural Contradictions of Capitalism.*

Many of America's greatest long-haul heroes were participants in the Black Freedom Struggle. In understanding this history, *Frederick Douglass: Prophet of Freedom* by David W. Blight, American Experience's *The Abolitionists*, Alyssa Battistoni's *n+1* essay "Spadework," racial justice crusader Ida B. Wells's work, and Martin Luther King Jr.'s books (in particular, *Stride Toward Freedom*, King's memoir of the Montgomery bus boycott) have been especially helpful to me.

I owe much of my understanding of local patriotism, community building, and solidarity to the Kentucky farmer-prophet Wendell Berry's essays, the philosopher Richard Rorty's *Achieving Our Country*, the online community Solidarity Hall, and the New York writer Bill Kauffman's localist manifesto, *Look Homeward, America*. It was Kauffman's book that first introduced me to the Catholic Worker founder Dorothy Day, who is perhaps America's greatest writer on and practitioner of dedication to the people right nearby. (It should be noted that Day's dedication to local hospitality did not stop her from agitating around national and international causes, too.) Mark T. Mitchell's writing on stewardship and Jeffrey Bilbro's writing on "convocation" were also inspiring to me. The two of them help helm *Front Porch Republic*, a little countercultural magazine on localism and stewardship of place.

You may have noticed that Jesuit spirituality is interwoven throughout much of the book. Three Jesuit priests—Father James F. Keenan, SJ, Father James Martin, SJ, and Father Brian McDermott, SJ—helped inform my understanding of the topic. Keenan's *Moral Wisdom: Lessons and Texts from the Catholic Tradition* and *The Works of Mercy: The Heart of Catholicism*, and Martin's *The Jesuit Guide to (Almost) Everything* are great reads.

Speaking of priests, the section on authenticity was influenced by the Catholic mystic and monk Thomas Merton's writing on the "false self" in his 1962 book, *New Seeds of Contemplation*. The lovely idea of celebration as "everybody making joy" is also Merton's, from his essay "The Street is for Celebration." And my idea of rediscovering commitment as a reforestation process was heavily influenced by Father Józef Tischner's *The Spirit of Solidarity*.

Two observations I had about organizing—campaign organizing, neighborhood organizing, and especially labor organizing—also inspired this book. The first is that the core work of organizing is encouraging people to make and keep long-haul commitments, both to one another and to a cause. The second is that lasting political change only comes from long-haul organizing—silver bullets and clever tricks are rare in history's successful causes. Two thinkers who helped me understand these observations better were the union organizer and scholar Jane McAlevey and the Pennsylvania community organizer Jonathan Smucker. McAlevey's *No Shortcuts: Organizing for Power in the New Gilded Age* and Smucker's *Hegemony How-To: A Roadmap for Radicals* are great places to start.

My thoughts on money were influenced by Michael Sandel's *What Money Can't Buy* and Michael Walzer's *Spheres of Justice*. Lewis Hyde's *The Gift* and Martin Buber's *I and Thou* greatly influenced my understanding of how market exchange can get in the way of dedication to particular people and communities. The mid-century critics Paul Goodman and Christopher Lasch, as well as the writer John Médaille, informed my understanding of the cultural consequences of the outsized scale of modern bureaucracies. The political scientist Theda Skocpol's *Diminished Democracy* introduced me to the useful idea of "membership" versus "management" in American civic life. And Jedediah Purdy's *For Common Things* helped me understand how institutions fit together like an ecosystem—and how institutional decline resembles ecosystem collapse.

Chris Hedges's *Death of the Liberal Class* does a great job explaining the problems with "neutral" institutions, and Chris Hayes's *Twilight of the Elites* does the same with modern meritocracy. Zach Wehrwein introduced me to the field of relational sociology. And Eleanor Duckworth's *The Having of Wonderful Ideas* sent me down the road to understanding that education is not the passive reception of information but rather the active exploration of ideas.

The importance of roots and the idea of our roots lying in the future is inspired by three thinkers. Simone Weil's *The Need for Roots* helps elucidate the role of roots in stabilizing our place in existence. In *The Next American Nation*, Michael Lind redefines the idea of a nation from a group that shares ancestors to a group that shares descendants—that a nation lives for its future, not its past. The philosopher Roberto Unger introduced me to the direct idea that our roots can lie in the future—and that in a democracy, "prophecy speaks louder than memory."

Unger, social scientist Robert Putnam, and civic advocate Ralph Nader are the three long-haul heroes who have most influenced me. Unger's radical Pragmatism—his assertion that "hope is the consequence of action" and his belief in "democratic experimentalism"— inspires my view that more widespread commitment to public projects will revitalize society. Putnam's epic studies on the importance of community building, social trust, and civic spirit changed the way I viewed our nation's problems—and are the reason I believe a culture of commitment is a prerequisite for democracy. And Nader's decades of dedicated work tirelessly crusading for the public interest showed me that it is supremely possible (with a little dedication) to turn abstract ideals into concrete action.

One final influence: You may notice a few song lyrics sprinkled throughout the book from the songwriter Joe Pug. (If I didn't have a good editor, there would have been twice as many.) Pug has a great commitment story of his own: On the night before his senior fall classes were to start, he dropped out of college, drove to Chicago, took up a job as a carpenter, and began pursuing his songwriting career at open mics around town. "I had a moment where I realized life is short and I knew where I wanted to be and I should just get there," he later said. Pug's lyrics are some of the best writing on the individual journey of finding your purpose in our confounding age. If I hadn't heard Pug's "Hymn #101" a decade ago, I'm not sure I would have written this book.

ACKNOWLEDGMENTS

Dedicated only exists because of the kindness and thoughtfulness of dozens of caring people.

This book began as a graduation speech. The speech only became a book because Carrie Cook saw the speech and decided to raise it up to the publishing world; my agent, Richard Pine, had faith that there was a full-length book inside the eight-minute speech; and my editor, Ben Loehnen, took a chance on this message. After I started this journey with them, they joked that we "were in for our own long haul together." I can't thank them enough for their guidance and encouragement in this process.

I am grateful to Jenn Walton for research assistance, Sonia Weiser for fact-checking, and my college roommate, Roger Hu, for first introducing me to the Jack Gilbert poem, "The Abnormal Is Not Courage." The book you are reading is much better than earlier drafts because Mike Bloomberg, Ian Corbin, Elias Crim, Zachary Davis, Collin Jones, Santiago Ramos, George Scialabba, Evan Warner, and Zach Wehrwein read early drafts and gave wise feedback.

For conversations over the years that led to this concept and support throughout the writing process, I am also grateful to Sparky Abraham, Kyla Alterman, Hannah Baumgardner, Vanessa A. Bee, Michael Costelloe, Bob Crowe, Emily Cunningham, Martin Drake, Mike Draskovic, Jonathan Finn-Gamino, Matt Geurtsen, Matt Gresko, Daniel Gross, Margaret Gallegos, Nora Gubbins, Michele Hall, Jonathan Herzog, Macabe Keliher, Lauren Kelleher, David Landy, Talia Lavin, Bob Mathews, Kathy Padilla, Alexandra Petri, Chris Pikrallidas, Ellen Pitera, Abbot Primate Gregory Polan, OSB, Ricky Porco, Alex Ramek, Cait Reilly, Brianna Rennix, John Richard, Nathan J. Robinson, Jim Roderick, Jamie Scharff, Karen Scharff, Ellen Selby, Michael Thornton, Roddie Turner, Paul VanKoughnett, Nathan Ward, Paige Whitlock, Heidi Whitman, and Jeff Williams. I am especially grateful to Allie Atkeson, Brennan Downey, Paula Gubbins, Scott Johnston, and Jon Staff, who have been talking through this project with me since it first began.

I am grateful to the dozens of long-haul heroes I interviewed in preparation for this book, who so kindly shared their commitment journey with me: Monte Anderson, Roger Beaman, Peggy Berryhill, Samuel Biagetti, Ken Burns, Tamaiko Chappell, Ernest Clover, Doris Crenshaw, Art Cullen, Sr. Mary Dacey, SSJ, Dave Eckert, Liz Fenwick, Pierce Freelon, Gabriela Grajeda, Ryan Gravel, Amy Jones, Sarah Kliff, Casper ter Kuile, Irene Li, Fr. Brian McDermott, SJ, Leslie Merriman, Annette Mills, Mark T. Mitchell, Gracy Olmstead, Andi Pettis, Joseph Phillips, Max Pollock, Alex Prewitt, Alex Ramek, Mickey Raphael, Mark Rivera, Jason Roberts, Rabbi Amy Schwartzman, Andy Shallal, Jason Slattery, Lee Vinsel, Lori Wallach, Karen Washington, Kimberly Wasserman, Sue Wessler, Sam Wohns, and Evan Wolfson. A number of others did not make it into the final draft, but I am grateful for their insights, which informed the book: Imam Naeem Baig of the Dar Al-Hijrah Islamic Center in Falls Church, CODEPINK founder Medea Benjamin, HarvestPlus founder Howdy Bouis, Homestretch director Christopher Fay, Maria and Ernie Flores, Mobile Loaves & Fishes founder Alan Graham, swimmer-turned-social worker Kennedy Higdon, Park Ranger and Buffalo Soldiers historian Shelton Johnson, plein air painter Rajendra KC, Durham organizer Sandra Korn, former National Bonsai Foundation president Felix Laughlin, prison journalist John J. Lennon, civil rights activist and educator Bob Moses, Masonic historian Mark Tabbert, and Camp Atwater CEO Henry Thomas III.

My sister, Rebecca Davis, is my commitment role model. I never cease to be inspired by her dedication, whether it's put to work making illuminating documentaries, unionizing her workplace, volunteering with mutual aid projects, mentoring students in her craft, or supporting her friends and family. I couldn't have written this book without her constant guidance, support, and example.

Though this book is about rebelling from the Culture of Open Options, I was blessed with being born into the Counterculture of Commitment. My parents, Mary Clare Gubbins and Shelton Davis, built a home that emphasized dedication to things bigger than self. In the spirit of the Franciscan dictum—"preach the Gospel; if necessary, use words"—they conveyed the importance of commitment to my sister and I through their daily example. In many ways, this book is the culmination of my decade-long journey to find the words to describe what is so special about my parents and people like them.

One of my interviewees, Monte Anderson, shared some wise advice about how to keep an even keel through a long haul: "When you're down, get grateful; when you're up, get humble." I am blessed to have a partner, Lark Turner, who fills me with gratitude and humility every day. She is the sharpest, savviest, and wisest editor out there—and after she spent dozens of late nights over the past year serving as a sounding board for ideas, punching up countless paragraphs, and helping shove this book across the finish line, it's accurate to say that *Dedicated* exists as much thanks to her dedication as it does to mine. While I was writing this book, Lark and I got married. It's the best commitment I will ever make.

ABOUT THE AUTHOR

PETE DAVIS is a civic advocate from Falls Church, Virginia. He works on projects aimed at deepening American democracy and solidarity. Pete is the cofounder of the Democracy Policy Network, a state policy organization focused on raising up ideas that deepen democracy. In 2015, he cofounded Getaway, a company that provides simple, unplugged escapes to tiny cabins outside of major cities. His Harvard Law School graduation speech, "A Counterculture of Commitment," has been viewed more than 30 million times. You can contact Pete at PeteDavis.org.